"You'll never meet a Christian who has never suffered loss, however great or small." So write Ted Kluck and Ronnie Martin in this compelling, needed book. Ted and Ronnie open their lives to let us see how God led them through painful loss. Their humility, honesty, and hopefulness in the power of the gospel will spur you to greater love for God.

—Collin Hansen, editorial director, The Gospel Coalition; author of *Young, Restless, Reformed: A Journalist's Journey with the New Calvinists*

Books Coauthored by Ted Kluck

FROM BETHANY HOUSE PUBLISHERS

Dallas and the Spitfire (Dallas Jahncke)
Finding God in the Dark (Ronnie Martin)
Dangerous (Caleb Bislow)

FINDING
GOD IN THE DARK

FINDING
GOD IN THE DARK

FAITH, DISAPPOINTMENT, AND THE STRUGGLE TO BELIEVE

TED KLUCK AND RONNIE MARTIN

BETHANY HOUSE PUBLISHERS

a division of Baker Publishing Group
Minneapolis, Minnesota

© 2013 by Ted Kluck and Ronnie Martin

Published by Bethany House Publishers
11400 Hampshire Avenue South
Bloomington, Minnesota 55438
www.bethanyhouse.com

Bethany House Publishers is a division of
Baker Publishing Group, Grand Rapids, Michigan

Printed in the United States of America

Library of Congress Cataloging-in-Publication Data
Kluck, Ted.
    Finding God in the dark : faith, disappointment, and the struggle to believe / Ted Kluck and Ronnie Martin.
      p. cm.
    Summary: "Popular author and award-winning musician help readers who struggle with doubt because of personal loss and disappointments"—Provided by publisher.
    Includes bibliographical references (p.).
    ISBN 978-0-7642-1082-2 (pbk. : alk. paper)
    1. Faith. 2. Disappointment—Religious aspects—Christianity. 3. Loss (Psychology)—Religious aspects—Christianity. I. Martin, Ronnie. II. Title.
BV4637.K54 2012
234′.23—dc23
                                        2012040443

Unless otherwise indicated, Scripture quotations are from The Holy Bible, English Standard Version® (ESV®), copyright © 2001 by Crossway, a publishing ministry of Good News Publishers. Used by permission. All rights reserved. ESV Text Edition: 2007

Scripture quotations identified NIV are from the Holy Bible, New International Version®. NIV®. Copyright © 1973, 1978, 1984, 2011 by Biblica, Inc.™ Used by permission of Zondervan. All rights reserved worldwide. www.zondervan.com

Cover design by Dan Pitts

Authors are represented by Wolgemuth & Associates.

13 14 15 16 17 18 19   7 6 5 4 3 2

For Kristin, who has forgiven much.

For everybody who hurts.

For Beth, and the hope that lies within.

Contents

Contents

Acknowledgments

From Ted

To the good friends in my life, in Christ: Ronnie Martin, Pat Quinn, Kevin DeYoung, Cory Hartman, Zach Bartels, Peeter Lukas. Your friendship has meant more this year than I could ever adequately express here.

To my agent, Andrew Wolgemuth, for being the coolest agent in this business, hands down, and for being a pro's pro.

To Mom and Dad for modeling this stuff to me, and for forgiving me, praying with me, and loving me in spite of all my flaws. You guys are the greatest. To Bonnie Skinner, for showing me an unbelievable amount of grace. May God bless you.

To University Reformed Church and Judson Memorial Baptist Church.

To Kristin, for forgiving much and loving me anyway. You're amazing, lovey.

From Ronnie

To Big T (you bring something nice to wear), Dan Allan, Jill Butler, Scott Burns, Robert Campbell, Tony Hall, David

Hegg, Bob Kauflin, Glenn Pickett, Rich Policz, Mark Spansel, Joseph Stigora, Nathan Wells, Danny Wright, and the Martins, the Devores, and the Harrisons—I need all of you, dear friends, so please keep texting me.

To Andrew Wolgemuth for absolutely everything, and Andy McGuire for grace, support, and encouragement. Expect Christmas cards forever.

To Ashland Grace Church—okay, we'll keep the organ.

To my wife, Melissa, and daughter, Beth—my two favorite people in the whole world.

Author's Note

Everybody Hurts

TED KLUCK

I've always hated the song "Everybody Hurts" by R.E.M. As a band, they always struck me as overly whiny and weaselly. R.E.M. was the guy in the perfect thrift-store ironic T-shirt, trying to find himself. Or the girl at the bookstore who was trying too hard to look casual. I'm from the middle of a cornfield (Hartford City, Indiana), and singing about how "everybody hurts" just seems soft, self-indulgent, and pointless.

But the thing is, everybody does hurt. Life (thirty-six years and counting) has shown me this. I've felt pain caused by others and, what's worse, my own sin has *caused* mental, physical, and emotional pain in others. Everybody hurts, and sometimes because of me. And in the church we sometimes expect people to just shrug and say, "Well, it's all part of God's plan," which isn't necessarily untrue, but it's a response that strikes me as a little inhuman and, if Scripture is to be believed, *unspiritual*. Job rent his garments and screamed, and the Bible said he was without sin in that particular situation. Jesus sweat blood in the garden. He didn't just skip to the cross saying, "Hey, I know how this is going to work out, so it's all good." Pain is real, and it's not necessarily unspiritual to acknowledge it. This book, in part, is an acknowledgment of pain and a reflection on what to do with it. My chapters are narrative in nature. By the ripe old(ish) age of thirty-six, one of the things I've learned about myself is that this, for better or worse, is how I write. This is a book about finding God in the dark. My chapters, in particular, will tell the stories of my "dark"—losing an adoption; experiencing professional failure; and then ultimately, by a movement of the Holy Spirit, confronting my own dark, sinful heart. Now, looking back, I am filled with thankfulness for these events because they are the events that God ordained for me to bring me into closer, deeper communion with Him. But in the midst of them. there was great pain.

Still, a temptation in reading a book like this, and narratives like these, would be to say, "Yeah, but Kluck hasn't gone through _____. He hasn't gone through what *I'm* going through." I know this will be a temptation because I've said similar things myself about stories that belonged to other people. "Yeah, but . . ."

I fully and openly acknowledge that there are many people who have gone through things that are much harder than the things I describe on these pages. But what's worth acknowledging, I think, is that these are the circumstances that God put *me* through in a particular time, and a particular place, for a particular purpose (my good and His glory). I've tried to re-create them as accurately as possible, even though the process was, at times, more than a little painful. If you're in Christ, you can trust that God is doing, and will do, the same for you in your circumstances. I've also tried to include

Scripture that's practical and relatable—the kinds of Scriptures you can pray through when you can't seem to find the words or energy to pray on your own.

One of the things I've always struggled with in life is listening to spiritual input from anyone whom I hadn't perceived as having gone through "deep waters." My hope and prayer for this book is that by reading about my deep waters, you can love and trust God more through yours.

Humbly, in Christ,

Ted Kluck

Introduction

RONNIE MARTIN

It's early on a Saturday morning as I sit down to write this intro, which I've decided to do in the somewhat cold, lifeless confines of my recording studio. I say lifeless because I'm surrounded by sparse birchwood walls, a gunmetal gray door, some strategically placed track lighting, and absolutely no windows. A vast array of knobs, switches, and meters that resemble an old laboratory from a science fiction movie in the 1960s are my only companions. For recording the kind of music I do, it's a perfectly designed space. There's no outside noise, outside light, or outside distraction coming in. Nobody else has any access unless I unlock the door and let them in. For all intents and purposes, I exist in total isolation when I'm in my studio, without any influence whatsoever from the outside world.

I think this may be an apt picture of how it feels when questions of faith, doubt, and unbelief come pressing into our hearts and minds. We feel detached, isolated, and alone. We feel neglected and wonder if God remembers that we're still His children. Sometimes we question whether He even exists at all.

Most of us don't need an introduction to any of these questions. As Tom Cruise once remarked in his Oscar-nominated role in *Jerry Maguire,* "We live in a cynical world. A cynical, cynical world."

He wasn't wrong.

The roots of doubt and unbelief are buried deep within the soil of our culture. From the first time the devil asked the question "Did God really say. . .?" to Eve in the garden, what he really did was call Eve to cynically question the love, goodness, trustworthiness, and reliability of God. To question His sovereignty. As we find ourselves mired in doubt and unbelief, we're simply grasping for an answer to the same question: "Did God really say . . . ?"

What Ted and I hope to do is explore the heart of this crucial question, a question that puts the goodness of God and the intent of His heart to the test. We'll do it by sharing with you some of the ordinary, everyday stories that make up the majority of our day-to-day lives. We realize that most of us don't face earth-shattering, death-defying moments that propel us headlong into severe doubts over God's goodness on a daily basis. For many of us, doubt and unbelief can be subtle poisons that gradually inoculate us over time from seeing the evidence of God's grace working steadily in our families, jobs, relationships, and futures. It's only when we begin to see, understand, and believe that God is truly at work in the fabric of every intricate detail of our lives that the dim light of doubt and unbelief gives way to the bright light of hope in Him.

> Light dawns in the darkness for the upright; he is gracious, merciful and upright.
>
> Psalm 112:4

It's after we find God in the dark that we realize He was already there.

1

You Gotta Have Faith

*The Source of Unbelief
(or the Struggle to Believe
When Life's Falling Apart)*

TED KLUCK

Gotta make it to heaven, for going through hell.

—50 Cent, "Gotta Make It to Heaven"

Cast all your anxieties on him because he cares for you.

—1 Peter 5:7 NIV

Hell hath no fury like a Ukrainian hallway.

Ukrainian hallways are dark and cold, strewn with trash, and smelling like some combination of urine, fried food, and garbage. A clichéd single lightbulb socket is either populated

19

by a broken lightbulb, or is hanging empty (likely stolen by one of the tenants).

These observances were all swirling in my mind as I crawled on my hands and knees back into my tiny apartment after a mild electrocution at the electrical box in the hallway—a box whose wires hadn't been looked at or manipulated since Stalin. My wife was crying. This was week one of a six-week stay in Ukraine. It was going to be a long stay.

When adopting in Ukraine, you are often told some pretty sketchy things that you just have to trust. Like you're told to be down on the street corner in five minutes to meet your ride, or you're told to strap twenty-large in cash around your waist—out of which you will be paying drivers, bribes, office workers, and all manner of people who will be converting and spending your American dollars. It's like being in a movie written by somebody else but starring you. Adopting abroad is an exercise in faith—in the people facilitating, the process, and God's sovereign plan.

My wife and I were in Kiev working on adopting the little boy who would become our second son, Maximilian Dmitri Kluck. Sometime during the first week we were told that Maxim had a sister named Anastasia, and that we could fill out paperwork that would allow us to come back a year later and adopt her too. We didn't know how we would fund the venture, but we said yes and cried tears of joy for the daughter we'd always hoped and prayed for that the Lord seemed to be providing.

Driving to the orphanage each day to see Maxim was an adventure in nausea control. Our driver, Vadim, had a penchant for stepping on and off the gas pedal often. This, coupled with big-city air pollution (Kiev—about the size of Chicago population-wise, but way less clean), made us sick to our stomachs nearly every day. Still, we saw so much on those drives. We visited a courthouse that was painted the exact same shade of pink as Pepto-Bismol. We saw beautiful centuries-old buildings stacked right next to newish depressing, concrete Soviet-era apartment buildings that looked like parking garages. The latter was the kind of building we called "home." I would stand at the window smoking cigarettes each night (hey, they were fifty cents a pack—it made good economic sense) and watch rats run out from beneath the building. That's entertainment!

The orphanage was a drab civic-ish building[1] located in an outlying town called Boyarka. Each day we walked into a dark (either all of the lightbulbs were burned out, or they were intentionally turned off to save money) room that featured a desk (always empty) and a really sad-looking[2] pile of plastic kids' toys. We would just stand there stupidly until someone came out to help us, because there were certain (read: most) areas of the orphanage into which we were forbidden to go. There were apparently things happening that they didn't want us to see.

One morning they brought her to us, but only for a moment.

Anastasia looked like Cindy Lou Who from *How the Grinch Stole Christmas*. She was tiny, two years old, blonde, and had little sloppy-yet-adorable pigtails. She had just been woken from a nap and was crying, but we had a moment to bond with her and take a picture. A picture that we would look at and pray over in the months to come. We were assured that the papers we filled out would make her ours, and we left Ukraine a month later (and many thousands of dollars lighter) with sweet Maxim Dmitri, and with the dream of returning in a year for his sister.

1. Think of the most depressing civic building you can imagine in America (like a Department of Motor Vehicles office), and then go a few steps worse.
2. Like the kind you see leftover at the end of garage sales.

Boulevard of Broken Dreams

The intervening months brought a lot of change. It was an adjustment to get used to two little boys in our house, as six years prior we had adopted Tristan Volodymyr Kluck, now eight, from another city in Ukraine. Tristan was strong as an ox—big, fast, outgoing, and aggressive. His brother, Maxim, was tiny, skinny, quiet, and malnourished, but as sweet as a little lamb. The two were quite a pair, and were soon thick as thieves. Tristan would do anything for his little brother.

All the while we guarded our hearts, knowing the craziness that was Ukrainian bureaucracy. But as the months went by, we slowly let our guard down. We began the herculean task of paperwork and fund-raising for Anastasia's adoption. We had a huge mom-to-mom sale at our church, and a big fund-raising night called Kluckstock, which featured a silent auction, a dessert buffet (prepared by my talented wife), and karaoke.[3] There was a lot of joy in the air. Fear of the unknown (and financial anxiety), but also pure joy. The Lord seemed to be moving mountains as our church rallied to bring this little girl into our home—a home where she would hear the gospel and be lovingly welcomed into a thriving local church. It seemed, to us, to be all good.

Then we got the call.

There's always a call. It came from the lady who had taken over the Ukraine program at our stateside adoption agency, and it was a lady who, honestly, neither Kristin nor I were crazy for. She was short and brusque which, ironically, made her a lot like a Ukrainian woman. Except that she was an American.

She dispassionately told us that due to a "change in some legislation"[4] in Ukraine, Anastasia was being adopted by a

---

3. Featuring yours truly belting out such hits as "Working for the Weekend" by Loverboy and "I Don't Wanna Miss a Thing" by Aerosmith.

4. This is shorthand for a bribe by a family with deeper pockets than ours.

Ukrainian family. We had, that very morning, started hanging girls' clothes in the closet of the room that would have been hers. We were already preparing to go back to Ukraine in a few months to get her. My wife sobbed angry tears and I tried to comfort her as well as I could . . . but words were no comfort.

Our contact at the adoption agency said that there was "nothing we can do," even as we tried advocating through lobbyists and politicians. Finally I penned an impassioned letter to the adoptive family. It may or may not have been the right thing to do:

Dear Family Adopting the Biological Sister of Our Adopted Son,

Forgive me for not knowing your names. To us you're just the subject of a very depressing phone call from our caseworker at Bethany Christian Services. To us you're just the couple who are negating the legal documents we signed last year in Ukraine during the adoption of Maximilian (our son), stating that we would be able to come back in a year and adopt Anastasia (his biological sister).

My name is Ted and my wife's name is Kristin. We've adopted two boys from Ukraine, ages seven and four. We're a very average American family—I write books and teach college English classes, and my wife works in the home raising these two energetic boys, whom we love dearly. Oddly, though, we have some things in common with you. We've both been to the selfsame orphanage in Boyarka, on the outskirts of Kiev, and have both fallen in love with the same vulnerable little girl there. We spent weeks in that orphanage—in the dark lobby, the even darker playroom, and the little playground out back, getting to know our sweet Maxim, and learning that he had a sister in the very same orphanage. One day they let us meet her and take her picture, and asked us to sign documents stating that we would indeed be adopting her. Documents that, they assured us, would protect us from this very situation.

We looked at that picture of her and prayed over it for the last year.

According to the depressing phone call we recently received, several families, like you, had expressed interest in her, but the orphanage rightly explained that there was an American couple (us) in line to adopt her once she was officially on the registry. But you persisted enough to have signed some other paperwork that has rendered our paperwork null and void. Let me say that I don't blame you for falling in love with her. If she's anything like her brother, she is happy, kind, quick to smile, and slow to anger.

What you are doing is not illegal, apparently, but still feels unspeakably mean.

Let me share a quick story. Knowing how things work in international adoptions (at times completely unpredictable and subject to change on a whim), we had a feeling something like this might happen. So we guarded our hearts against it for several months. But recently my wife decided to start hanging girls' clothes in the closet in our extra bedroom. We had gotten close enough to the adoption to allow ourselves to begin to hope and to stop guarding our hearts.

Let me close by asking you a question: Is this really how you want to enter into a lifelong relationship with this child, knowing that you broke the hearts of another family and separated her from her biological brother? Our hearts will heal eventually. We trust and love and believe in a sovereign God who gives and takes away. But still, this sucks.

I would love for you to look me in the eye and tell me, in person,[5] all of the reasons why it's necessary, in an entire country full of orphans, for you to adopt the girl we've been hoping and praying for as our daughter.

Let me be the first to acknowledge the fact that we don't expect this letter to do anything. I'll be shocked if it ever reaches you, but in a weird way I feel better for having written it. If you've gotten to this point in the process, you may very well not be the kind of people who would be moved by a letter like this. But please know that there are real people on the other end of this process. If I were a better Christian, I would say that I forgive you and I'm praying for you. But I don't think I have, and I'm not. But I am praying for your daughter.

Sincerely,
Ted and Kristin Kluck

The letter did nothing. And neither did our prayers that God would work a miracle in the situation and unite Anastasia with her brother. The result was heartache, pain, depression, doubt, cynicism, and *unbelief.*

Help My Unbelief

In my life the core trigger for unbelief and cynicism has been broken dreams and unmet expectations of which I have had many, but probably no more than the average person. There have been book deals that have fallen through,[6] a semi-promising football career lost to injury, broken promises from Christians, and just plain old disappointment at wanting

5. What I really wanted was to show this guy an up-close view of my fist.
6. Too many to recount.

something desperately and not being able to have it. This is part of the human condition. It's the part that makes you cynical. It's the part that makes you just want to black out and fall asleep for a long, long time.

It has been those scenarios, like Anastasia, in which God shows us something that on the surface looks so airtight and amazing it *has* to be from Him. This is at least what we tell ourselves as we try to understand God's sovereign will. To see it taken away is, quite simply, heartbreaking. It brings with it anger, grief, and a loss of hope.

My tendency in the wake of Anastasia was to expect bad things to happen. To ask God if He put me on this earth just so that He could give me a beating. I stopped believing in His sovereign plan and started feeling like a punching bag. My human reaction was to become cynical and wary.

The father with the sick, demon-possessed child in Mark 9 must have felt the same way. Being a father in those days probably wasn't a whole lot different from being a father now. You love your child in a desperate, gut-level way. A take-a-bullet-for-this-person kind of way. Imagine your child is sick—possessed by an evil spirit, the text tells us—and you've tried everything to help him. People are looking at you funny because you've got a weird kid. "What did he do to deserve that?" they mutter under their breath, all the while wishing you well in public. The condition takes its toll on your home, your marriage, and your ability to think, eat, and sleep normally. You enter survival mode—completing only those tasks that are essential for life—and live joylessly from day to day. Fatherhood is tough anyway, but it's harder when you're taking an emotional beating from life and circumstances. You have trouble believing and hoping.

So the man in Mark 9 says, "If you can do anything, take pity on us and help us." "'If you can'?" said Jesus. "Everything is possible for one who believes." "I believe," the man said. "Help me overcome my unbelief."[7]

This is an example of a struggling, weary, beaten, and scarred—but still viable—faith. A faith that's on the ropes but still standing. It's an example of how to believe in the face of great trial. The man not only trusts Jesus with his child, but with his unbelief as well. He is casting all his anxieties on Him, who cares for him.

In the wake of Anastasia, I was wracked with anxieties. Financial anxiety over the money we'd lost in the adoption, professional anxiety, and most of all personal anxiety over my inability to feel love for a Lord who would take this away from us. My wife was hurting as well. She was retreating from the women at church, and she even had a hard time talking to me about what she was experiencing. Infertility and a failed adoption were shaking her faith to the core.

I knew in my head that God was real, and I even believed that He loved me. I just wanted, and needed, to feel it. I remember a road trip we took following Anastasia's loss. We were so frustrated—tapped out mentally, physically, and financially—that we were both in tears. I was trying to personally carry and deal with all of my anxieties, and was failing miserably. I was being driven to my knees, again, by a God who loved me and cared for me. At the time I questioned two essential biblical truths—that God was good, and that He loved me. I was refusing to cast my anxieties on Him, because I struggled to fully trust Him not to hurt me again. I believed in His sovereignty. . . . I believed that He had ordained Anastasia's loss, and that it wasn't the . Enemy, as some would suggest. I believe that God is ruler of all, even the Enemy. Though, to be honest, it would have been easier to be mad at the devil. I think being mad at God,

7. Mark 9:22–24

in the absence of hope and trust, is the darkest, loneliest place of all.

I still believed, but I needed help in my unbelief. I needed to cast my anxieties on Him, who cared for me. Scripture had given me a framework for praying through my unbelief, but I was refusing to see it and use it. David, the psalmist, sums up this framework perfectly in Psalm 13—a dark and tormented, but ultimately hopeful, picture of believing through suffering:

> How long will you hide your face from me?
> How long must I wrestle with my thoughts
>   and day after day have sorrow in my heart?
>   How long will my enemy triumph over me?
>
> Look on me and answer, LORD my God.
> Give light to my eyes, or I will sleep in death,
>   and my enemy will say, "I have overcome him,"
>   and my foes will rejoice when I fall.
>
> But I trust in your unfailing love;
> my heart rejoices in your salvation.
> I will sing the LORD's praise,
>   for he has been good to me. (NIV)

It rained and we drove and cried. Music didn't sound good. Food didn't taste good. The world seemed dark and bleak. Life seemed a series of disappointments, peppered with occasional rays of hope. I silently hoped that my wife still loved me in the midst of all this failure, but I think I also wouldn't have blamed her if she didn't.

2

How Soon Is Now?

When God's People Question the Reliability of God

RONNIE MARTIN

It's 10:00 a.m. and I'm sitting in the parking lot at Starbucks waiting to meet a friend. I see that he hasn't arrived, so I put my car in park, turn up the A/C, and start rummaging through my collection of overplayed CDs. I'm already slightly agitated because one, I'm the son of a Navy man, so being on time was a rule to be followed under penalty of death growing up in the Martin household. Secondly, this particular individual was usually twenty minutes late on his best day, and today was not one of them as I looked at my phone and saw that it was now 10:45. I was burning inside as I frantically texted my wife, letting her know how unbelievable it was that I was still sitting here and how badly the rest of the day was going to play out now because of it.

At the root of my frustration was the fact that I simply couldn't rely on this person. Although he was generally nice and I enjoyed his company when we were together, his relentless tardiness had begun to make me feel like he really didn't care about me at all. It should come as no surprise that our friendship eventually dwindled as a result.

Whether we like it or not, we are fiercely dependent people. As much as some of us like to think that we're doggedly independent, the reality is that we're all forced to rely on others to do what they say they're going to do and be who we think they are. Our lives depend on it. When people let us down, we experience a breakdown. Trust becomes a commodity, and our next step is to take matters into our own hands. We may give people a second chance, but we're going to question their reliability until they've shown us they can be relied on once again.

Unfortunately, we treat God like we treat people.

Here are just a few examples of God's people questioning the reliability of God:

1. Moses losing his cool and bashing a rock to make a water fountain.
2. Jacob playing dress-up to steal the birthright from his brother Esau.
3. Jonah deciding to hit a cruise line after God told him to go preach somewhere else.
4. Peter chopping a guy's ear off when the mob came to arrest Jesus.

The reason we take things into our own hands is that we don't believe God's hands are really at work. Or in my case, it can be like what C. S. Lewis wrote: "We're not necessarily doubting that God will do the best for us; we are wondering how painful the best will turn out to be."[1]

1. Walter Hooper, ed., *The Collected Letters of C. S. Lewis, Volume 3* (New York: Harper Collins, 2007).

Whatever end of the receiving line of doubt you find yourself on, it all stems from a fundamental disbelief that God is as good as He says He is. We can affirm it in our minds and say it with our mouths, but until it penetrates our hearts it will never transform our lives. We sing "Jesus Paid It All" on Sunday, but in our fiercest battles with doubt and unbelief we try to buy it back. Second Peter 1:3 says, "His divine power has granted to us all things that pertain to life and godliness, through the knowledge of him who called us to his own glory and excellence." It says it all right there in black and white, clear as crystal. We're not lacking anything that we need. Our heavenly Father is our great provider, but we often view Him as our great *denier*. We believe He has granted *some things* to us that pertain to life and godliness, but all the things that we actually want? Not so much.

When I was a kid, my dad loved when I asked him to give me an idea of what I might be getting for Christmas. In the weeks leading up to the big day, he'd play this little game with me where I begged and pleaded for clues, and he would frustratingly tease me with vague, misleading hints. By the time we were done with all the back-and-forth, I was convinced that there was no way I was getting what I really wanted for Christmas. I'd make the long walk (thirty feet) back to my bedroom feeling dejected and depressed, while my pops gleefully sat there smirking on the couch, relishing the victory he achieved over a game of wits with a nine-year-old. It would all be worth it on Christmas morning when I received the gift(s) I asked for and he could bask in the glow of my joyously surprised reaction.

I'm convinced we view our heavenly Father the same way. We think He's playing a game of cosmic give-and-take, and what He's giving us can't be what we really want. In many cases it's not, but that's because our definition of life and godliness is not what He really wants for us. It was inevitable that I'd receive a boring, horrible sweater or two for Christmas every year, but it wasn't always at the expense of the things I wanted. Ironically, I'd still be wearing those sweaters a year later, but those toys I couldn't live without were long gone, which is why I asked for more. What God really wants is for us to taste and see His goodness in all things, but many times the things that help us the most are the ones we cherish the least, because they can hurt like heck.

Great hearts can only be made by great troubles.

Charles Spurgeon

For you know that the testing of your faith produces steadfastness.

James 1:3

The Boy With the Thorn in His Side

It had been a brutal road trip in the Pacific Northwest. Twenty years of national and international touring only made it harder. Concerts that had normally been well attended in places like Portland, Bremerton, and Seattle had been dismal. Morale was low between my drummer Rob and me, and although this wasn't the first time we'd found ourselves wallowing in this type of pride-sucking, ego-deflating, on-the-road drama, you never truly get used to it. The one bright spot had been attending a Sunday service at a Mars Hill satellite church in Olympia, Washington. It had been encouraging to hear Mark Driscoll preach God's Word and hear the worship band play more out of tune than we'd ever been, but I was still squirming with impatience as I contemplated the final two days of our tour schedule. Of course people were going through worse things in the world, but the constant liveli-hood of my *art* was at stake, so at minimum I was feeling a dull, inconsolable ache, because numbers don't typically lie: People either buy tickets to watch you play, or they don't. This tour had been an acute case of the latter.

The only thing left on the agenda the following day was a meeting I had scheduled with my record label in Seattle. My contract was up and we were going to talk renegotiation, or at least I hoped so. The concern I had was due to the fact that though we had never been big sellers on the label, we had somehow stayed dear to them through loyalty, hard work, and an always welcome dose of critical/artistic acclaim. None of which helped them pay the bills, of course, but sure helped us pay ours.

I was nervous the next day as I sat down to lunch with the president and VP of the label, and rightfully so, as they proceeded to inform me that everything I had come to enjoy in my previous contract was not going to be extended to my next one. Though not entirely unexpected, I felt the air leave my lungs. After thirteen years, the writing was finally on the wall: The financial support I had come to depend on would be coming to an end. The cash advances I had received as an artist who had been given 100 percent control of his vision and output were being cut off. The dream had died. Everything must pass . . . including a good portion of my yearly income.

I boarded my plane the next morning feeling knotted up, lost, and alone.

Did God have a plan in all this? I'm sure He did, and I'm sure Mark Driscoll even mentioned something about it when they broadcasted his sermon in Olympia on Sunday, but I don't know if I gave myself even a moment to consider the truth of that fact. For all intents and purposes, I had become a functioning unbeliever. Sure, at any moment I could pledge my allegiance to the Christian faith, but the response of my heart in this life-changing moment was akin to those who used phrases like "the man upstairs" and "the good Lord above." Whatever faith I did claim to have was experiencing a seismic shift, and was being exposed as paper thin and easily torn. Instead of a faith that was "rooted and built up in him" (Colossians 2:7), I had placed all my hope in the talents He had given me and the identity I had drawn from them. Like Tim Keller says, "Our need for worth is so powerful that whatever we base our identity and value on we essentially 'deify.' We will look to it with all the passion and intensity of worship and devotion, even if we think ourselves as highly irreligious."[2]

That about sums it up. My art had become my God. All of my passion and intensity was directed at the thing I pulled my identity from and put all my value on. I know this because the moment there was a chance it could be taken from me, my entire world imploded. I didn't know who I was, I didn't feel like life had meaning, and I was immediately plunged into darkness, despair, and doubt. I was so deliriously and crazy in love with my persona as an artist that the thought of losing that identity felt like the death of a loved one. And that came one month later.

I Know It's Over

The sun had barely come up when we crested the back hills of Rancho Santa Margarita and made our way down into the upper middle class Mecca of San Juan Capistrano, California. No, I wasn't taking the family for an early morning joyride through the sun-drenched hills of Southern California . . . this was a little more serious. At 4:00 a.m. I'd been

2. Tim Keller, *The Reason for God* (New York: Dutton, 2008), Kindle edition, chapter 10.

awakened by the sound of my Blackberry buzzing like a bad dream. It was Mom. Dad had been rushed to the hospital. He couldn't feel his legs. She sounded unusually calm for herself but said we should come as soon as possible. My two brothers and two sisters were on the way. I stared into the dark for a few minutes, trying to contemplate the surreal quality of the moment. My wife, Melissa, clung to my arm, looking wide-eyed and fearful. Truth be told, it was a call I knew I'd get someday, and I always wondered where I'd be when I got it. It had nothing to do with morbidity, but more with dread, and I realized I had hit the nail on the head as the knots started clenching in my stomach.

My family was the last to get to Mission Hospital, which reminded me of how my mom always commented that we were fashionably late to family functions. I always wanted to tell her we weren't trying to be fashionable, but being late helped us function a little better with the family. It hasn't always been an easy task.

It was a strange sight to see all my brothers and sisters in one room together, much less the waiting room at Mission Hospital. Although we occasionally bumped into one another on a holiday now and again, it was kind of rare when we were all together in the same place anymore.

I made eye contact with the sibs and quickly sat down next to Mom to get the lowdown on Dad. She didn't know much. Turned out nobody did. The doctors said it was something to do with his heart but that it wasn't a heart attack. In classic Martin fashion, everybody was speculating wildly, which always drove me a little crazy.

At one point a bearded, red-haired chaplain named Walter came into the room and introduced himself to everyone. Nice guy. He had a calm, reassuring way about him like a lot of these guys do, but was even more personable than I could've hoped. He told us he'd be the one checking in with the doctor and keeping us in the loop, which of course brought on more questions, none of which he had any answers for.

As I settled into my seat and started surveying the scene, I became fascinated as I watched Walter "work the room." He casually answered everybody's questions, joked around with the kids, and seemed genuinely concerned and interested in whatever was being discussed. I couldn't help but wonder how on earth he did the job he did. Who wakes up one morning and decides they want to be the guy at the hospital who gets to say "Sorry, but he ain't gonna make it"? Not fun.

A couple hours later, and with precious little communication from the doctors, it was somehow decided that they were probably going to keep Dad for a day or two, and hopefully we'd all be able to see him before we left. We just needed to get the word that everything was okay and we could be on our way. I thought it was a strange assumption given how little information we'd been given, but I decided to put my glass-half-empty tendencies aside for the moment.

It wasn't too long before Walter came back in and made a beeline for Mom. I knew something was wrong the second he put his hand on her arm.

"Lorraine, I just spoke with the doctors. . . . Jay has died."

The odd things you remember from life's defining moments. I remember having the sensation of falling, but not the kind of falling you feel in a dream. This was much more immediate and had a very definable beginning and end, like something making contact with something else. It was like something breaking, I guess, but it went beyond that. Some of the older grandkids started crying. My mom seemed frozen in a state of disbelief for a second before she put her head in her hands and started saying, "Jay, I'm sorry," over and over. My older brother, Keith, and younger brother, Jason, dashed into the hallway, wanting to be alone to try to conceal their emotions. I don't remember what anyone else did. But I remember Walter. He was there, kneeling next to my mom, his hand on her back, weeping bitterly alongside her. I was stunned. This was a person we had known for only four hours. If you would've come into the room at that moment, you would have thought he was one of my dad's sons.

I realized after a few minutes that although my eyes were tearing and I felt a strange emptiness in my heart, my gaze had been fixed on Walter. He left my mom's side and went around the room, talking to my sisters, consoling the grandkids, somehow fitting in better to our family dynamic than anyone ever had. At one point my brother Keith returned and started telling Walter about the kind of person our dad was, and how much he would've liked him. Keith told him that Dad was a "Christian man" (he was), and described how devoted to his friends and family he had always been (it was true). Walter just stood there looking deeply into my brother's eyes, listening intently to everything he was saying while responding with understanding nods and gestures. It made me sad to think about the volatile relationship Keith and my dad had shared together. They'd not had an easy run. How I wished Dad could've heard some of the nice things his son was saying about him now.

The room settled into a dreary calm. Family members started to move about in shock, not really knowing what to do next. At some point I approached Walter to thank him for everything he had done. Tears were slowly streaming down my face, and my voice was cracking and shaky. For some reason I felt the need to communicate that his kindness had touched a cord inside of me. Somehow, seeing him pour his heart out to strangers like us had made me hopeful instead of hopeless. Maybe what I saw was a picture of our Savior in those desperate moments—I don't know. One thing I do know is that God had divinely appointed this chaplain to be at Mission Hospital the morning my dad was going to die of a heart aneurism. It was a moment I've revisited in my mind many times since. In fact, it's usually the only thing I think about when my thoughts drift back to that morning.

Cemetery Gates

A week passed. I stood under the big, shady tree on my front lawn and waved good-bye as the last of the family drove on down the road. It had been a long day and I was exhausted. The sun was just going down on the horizon, and I closed my eyes, letting the warm August breeze wash over my tired face like invisible waves. I retraced my steps over the past week.

Five hours earlier I had delivered the eulogy at Dad's funeral. There were almost sixty people there. I doubted I would have had half as many. I wrote something quickly and delivered the first draft. It just felt right. I made it almost to the end before the emotions of the moment overcame me. I was too sad to be embarrassed.

My friend (and pastor) Robert officiated the funeral. His depth of understanding and compassion overwhelmed me, much like the chaplain had done the week before. I guess I felt cared for in a way I'd not experienced up to this point. It probably says a lot that it shocked me so much.

Another friend (and pastor), named Kimani, showed up too. He walked up the grass knoll toward the pavilion where we gathered, wearing a dark blue suit, already sweating in the merciless summer heat. I didn't know he was coming. He didn't even know my dad. I felt humbled and unworthy of his kindness. And somehow ashamed.

I thought back to the Sunday morning before, as my wife and I walked into our church foyer, hoping we wouldn't see anybody we knew before services started. Someone from our small group was already waiting for us and led me and Melissa to a row where everybody from the group was sitting together. This was something that had never happened. It made my wife cry.

After we sat down, Pastor Mark walked on stage to deliver the announcements. I hadn't gotten to know him too well. Before he started, he mentioned that there were some in the congregation who were suffering heartbreak and that the Lord was close to them. It made me cry. I wouldn't find out until years later that Mark had lost his dad as a teenager.

There's nothing quite like the church being the church. It's one of the ways God restores us.

My mind continued to drift over the sad events that unfolded during one of the hardest months of my life. I wouldn't realize until later how impactful and influential these people would be to the reigniting of my faith, which had grown stagnant and stunted. The process had finally begun. God had decided enough was enough. I was being broken down in preparation for rebuilding. It felt lonely and confusing.

Paint a Vulgar Picture

> The LORD is near to the brokenhearted and saves the crushed in spirit.
>
> Psalm 34:18

A broken heart and crushed spirit. I knew these two emotions well on an artistic level. In fact, I had written hundreds of songs as the result of them, but my spiritual life had been almost completely devoid of the experience. The words *broken* and *crushed* were how I typically felt when I wasn't getting my way or the kind of attention I felt I needed and deserved. As a guy who had essentially grown up in the church, I had grown calloused toward the all-loving, self-crushing power of the gospel. For all intents and purposes, the gospel was something I had simply assumed, meaning I had "conformed to a pattern of behavior and not been transformed by the power of the Holy Spirit."[3]

Yes, I believe the Lord had given me a new heart once upon a time, but after all these years it was operating at a very low pulse.

Our initial struggles with darkness and doubt don't have the benefit of hindsight. It is in our early bouts with distrust that we feel at our most alone, unable to compare the reality of our emotions and circumstances with anything else. If we take a closer look, we discover God taking painful yet drastic measures to destroy our idols, level our doubts, and show us the incomparable bluntness, brightness, and beauty of His grace. The experience is horrific. It's like losing a limb to a disease. It had to go to save your life, but now it feels like there's something missing because, well, there is. But living without it is what's enabling you to live at all.

> So we do not lose heart. Though our outer self is wasting away, our inner self is being renewed day by day. For this light momentary affliction is preparing for us an eternal weight of glory beyond all comparison, as we look not to the things that are seen but to the things that are unseen. For the things that are seen are transient, but the things that are unseen are eternal.
>
> 2 Corinthians 4:16–18

3. Matt Chandler, *The Explicit Gospel* (Wheaton, IL: Crossway, 2012), 14.

My inner self was wasting away because I was only content to focus on my outer self. Because of that, any affliction or heartbreak I did experience didn't feel light or momentary. Long before the downturns of this memorable summer, my life had become a series of dramatic exaggerations, fueled by how angry I was that I had to depend on others for my success, solutions, and standard of living. In truth, my anger was aimed directly at God. I was angry at the sovereign decisions He had made that had little to do with the decisions I preferred Him to make. I had developed eyes for the transient things right in front of my face, but had grown blind to the unseen, eternal things of God. Is that some kind of oxymoron? If something's unseen, how can we be blind to it? We're blind to it when we use the eyes of our flesh, not the eyes of our heart. The Holy Spirit supplies us with vision of the heart to see the unseen things of God.

> Having the eyes of your hearts enlightened, that you may know what is the hope to which he has called you.
>
> Ephesians 1:18

God wants us to glory in the hope of himself. He wants our eyes to be continually opened to see the evidence of His goodness. We don't have to look far. Our lives are saturated by it, but many times it's most visible in hindsight.

These Things Take Time

The story of Joseph is a cinematic backdrop like no other. We're talking about a spoiled, insensitive trust-fund baby, coddled by his daddy until his brothers have finally had enough of his insufferable bragging, and decide to throw him in a hole while they draw up plans on how to knock him off. They end up voting against murder but sell him into slavery, thinking he'd still be out of their hair for good.

Things start looking up for Joseph pretty quick in the slave trade when he lands a manager position thanks to his hard work and good behavior. Everything's going swimmingly until he gets framed on rape charges against his boss's wife. He ends up in jail but manages to land another managerial position. Along the way, he ends up helping another prisoner from the pharaoh's court get pardoned, who is so thankful that he—wait for it—forgets to tell pharaoh that Joseph was locked up under false charges. Two years later the guy's memory returns, and he tells the king he knows a guy who's good at interpreting dreams, because the pharaoh just had a doozy. They bring Joseph in, he interprets the dream, and proceeds to land the VP position for the entire nation of Egypt.

Okay, that's a condensed version for you, but you know what I always think when I read this? That the prime years of Joseph's life were savagely taken from him. Regardless of how lovely it all turned out, the guy happened to be almost forty by the time he got that VP gig. I don't see myself being okay with that. I don't see myself just slogging through, spending another cheery day in an Egyptian jail cell trusting that God has everything under His control and that He'll bring me to justice in His own good timing. No, I see myself agonizing over the lost years of my youth, wondering what might have been and why God had left me to waste away into nothing. I would want to know why He had been so unreliable.

Joseph saw things differently after he finally came face-to-face with his brothers so many years later. He recognized that God uses all things, including the sinful acts of men, to bring about His will and purpose.

As for you, you meant evil against me, but God meant it for good, to bring it about that many people should be kept alive, as they are today.

Genesis 50:20

God's actions are never arbitrary. His intentions are always for our good. His motivation is always for His glory. Because we don't possess that kind of divine, purposeful, and perfect intentionality, we sometimes forget that we know and can trust Someone who does.

The truth is that God takes drastic measures for us to have hearts that are transformed by His severe mercy and sovereign grace. Here's the thing: We're not told much about the personal pain Joseph experienced. We're not told of the sleepless nights he must have spent in isolation, gripped by emotional despondency while grasping hopelessly in the dark, trying to fathom why God was doing what He was doing, or whether He was even there. In hindsight, we tend to view figures like Joseph as emboldened, courageous pillars of the faith, but it's foolishness to think that the response of their hearts was any less weak and human than ours would be. What we do see is a God who uses very human experiences to change the hearts of His human vessels.

There Is a Light That Never Goes Out

Most of us really believe in the partial sovereignty of God. We believe He's doing work in our hearts and lives, but when problems and difficulties rear their ugly head, we feel it's time to take matters into our own hands, because God must have decided to take a break for a while. It's in these times that we live like functioning unbelievers and experience the hopelessness that God already saved us from. We end up responding like people who have *kind of* followed Christ, and whose crosses have *allegedly* been taken up and have been crucified with Him.

The irony of this is not missed on me as I look back on the year of my dad's death. The fact is that my faith had reached a moment of critical mass. The time had come for me to stop languishing in halfhearted religious and Christian posturing and start serving my Savior. The problem was that there were barriers in my life that needed to be dismantled and destroyed. I'm not saying God took my dad's life for this to happen, because only He knows our appointed times and the reasons for them. What I do know is that because of my dad's death, I was able to see the evidence of God's grace more clearly in my life. I had a death grip on my identity as an artist. I had a love affair with comfort, and I pursued almost whatever it took to keep it within the arms of familiarity. The light of Christ that had once shone brightly in my life was now dim, dull, and mostly unnoticeable. Even though I was a card carrying follower of Christ, I lacked any real evidence of the One I followed. It was through real pain, and the exposure of real sin in my life, that I was forced to have real reliance in Christ. There was no other way.

There is never an absence of God in our lives. I don't know what kind of doubts the apostle Paul must have had when he was chained in rat-infested dungeons, with rusted chains digging into his arms, not hearing the sound of human voices for days on end, wondering why on earth God was keeping him from accomplishing so much more ministry. We are given a clue to how Paul responded, though, and that was with prayer, singing, writing, and evangelism. We sometimes struggle to find God in the dark because we feel like our lives are passing before our eyes. But in reality, we're simply not opening our eyes to where God has placed us. Paul changed the world while he was locked up, writing letters that have altered the fabric of Christianity. It was never so dark in Paul's life that he allowed himself to believe that God was absent. Instead, he prayed for the eyes to see God's sovereign hand, a mind to comprehend His unending goodness, and a heart to overflow in gratefulness.

> The strength of patience hangs on our capacity to believe that God is up to something good for us in all our delays and detours.
>
> John Piper

3

How *You* Doin'?

Culture's Obsession With Self-Sufficiency

TED KLUCK

I have an iron will, and all of my will has always been to conquer some horrible feeling of inadequacy. . . . My drive in life is from this horrible fear of being mediocre.

—Madonna, pop star

With that first, two-hundred-dollar payday, Sonny had entered a world in which money was the kind and loving God of the ruling few, and the predestining subjugator of many.

—Nick Tosches, *The Devil and Sonny Liston*

There's a great guy in our church who, in addition to being, like, seven feet tall, is also the de facto lobby greeter. Has been for years. He hovers sort of mid-lobby, past the dual glass doors, but not all the way to the drinking fountains or the distinctive row of church mailboxes. (Distinctive in that there is something about the industrial-grade carpet, drinking fountains, and slender wooden mailboxes that just *says* "I'm in a suburban evangelical church.")

Anyway, this guy is super friendly and has taken it upon himself to personally greet everyone who comes into church— new or old. When life is "good" circumstantially, I enjoy greeting him, and I may even whack him on the back in a show of robust male solidarity. When life is "bad" circumstantially, I try to avoid him like the proverbial plague. I would rather take a beating than see him, smile, and suffer through the thirty seconds of small talk and lies before getting past him and into my seat, where I can hide to some degree. (You see, when you're in your seat, it's like there's a little force field of privacy around you. You can pretend to read the bulletin or, if you're really bold, you can just close your eyes.)

Caveat: My wife and I (mostly) love our church. I even wrote a book called *Why We Love the Church*, which for fifteen cultural minutes made me semi-famous in Reformed circles. Not coincidentally (I think), immediately following the release of that book, we entered into a years-long cycle of intense and painful struggle with our church, which hinged on personal intense, painful struggles, which we'll go into in more detail later (infertility and sin).

During those years we became *those* people. We became the people who are *in* the church but not *of* the church. The people who habitually slip in fifteen minutes late and who try like animals to bust out of the lobby as quickly as possible afterward. The lobby becomes a sort of video game that exists to be beaten. To be overcome. To be leveled-up. If we get out quickly, with a minimum of bad conversations, we win and lunch is fun. If we don't, we lose, and lunch (and probably the rest of the day or maybe even week) is unpleasant.

A short list of people to avoid in the lobby:

The "How *You* Doin'?" College Kid. This fun, fresh-faced student has just changed his major for the sixth time and/or has broken up or gotten back together with that special someone and just wants to tell you all about it. He asks how you're doing so that you can say "fine," and then he can quickly launch into his thing.

The "How Are You *Really* Doing" Lady. This lady has the best of intentions because she wants to go deep with you in the lobby, and she wants you to know that she wants to go deep. She does this by making constant, almost creepy eye contact and by placing her hand on your shoulder. She *really* wants to get the scoop on what's happening with you, and you may actually want to share your issues with this lady, but not while your kid is hanging off your arm and his Sunday school papers are falling out onto the floor.

The "How's Work Going" Guy. This guy asks everybody how work is going because work is going AWESOME for him! He's getting promoted, closing the deal, adding onto his house, and doing it all with a Jesus-fish on his bumper and a 4:00 a.m. men's Bible study on Thursday mornings. He is the man.

And here's a short (incomplete) list of issues that can make church difficult:

Infertility
Joblessness
Apostate Children
Marital Distress
Career Singleness

Depression/Anxiety

Sexual Issues—Abuse, Same-Sex Attraction, Transgenderism

Relational Stress

Family Dysfunction

Any Sickness That You Have Any Measure of Control Over (eating disorders, alcoholism, etc.)

Debt or Other Financial Crisis

As Christians, we're the ones who *say* we're pilgrims in an imperfect, sinful world. Yet we're the ones who want to go to church on Sunday as though our lives and ourselves are unblemished and unaffected by the blight of sin. It's been our experience that only the most *extreme* of challenges (public sin, death, etc.) cause church people to really become honest with each other.

I teach at a small Christian college in Michigan, and it's a gig that I absolutely love. At this particular school, all of my students are provided a laptop upon enrollment, and there is a great deal of faculty hand-wringing over the topic of laptops in the classroom. Most faculty outlaw them completely, paranoid that Facebook and fantasy sports will trump their lectures in importance and entertainment value (they're probably right). I love that my students have laptops and I encourage them to bring them to class, figuring that since they're technically adults, they'll be able to make semi-responsible choices about what they do in class. My only rule is that I retain final veto power over any photograph that is taken of me and posted to Facebook. I retain the right to make sure I look awesome (see: Vanity of vanities, all is vanity).

It's not news to anyone that we live in an extremely narcissistic culture. Facebook, Twitter, and the blogosphere have turned us all into our own best press agents. We post only the most clever, intriguing comments; we post only the best pictures; and we generally try to make all of our followers believe that we have handcrafted the most impressive of lives. We live for that little hit of ego that comes with logging in to find more friend requests or comments on our pictures.

Under the guise of "marketing," authors (myself included) will post a link to a favorable review or the Amazon link to one of our books. This is also done under the guise of "I just wanted to let you know . . ." We try to retain a sense of "aw-shucks" false humility about it, but we check back desperately, waiting for the well-wishes and congratulations to roll in. This never ceases to make me feel creepy. But I kept doing it for a long time.

In general, we all are spiritual self-promoters, trying to outdo one another by linking to the most intriguing or latest story to come out of the evangelical blogosphere. The blogosphere is reality television for people (conservative Christians) who consider themselves too good for reality television.

Not even that noblest of professions—stay-at-home mom—is immune to this sort of technological grandstanding. Status updates about perfect playdates or craft projects, or magazine-quality photographs of picture-perfect birthday parties induce lots of fawning compliments (and private eye-rolls) from other moms. Moms are the most underrated competitive people-group on earth. If I had to go to a rumble in a dark alley, I'd be sure to take a few stay-at-home moms with me.

Facebook can let your friends know what you're reading, what you're watching, what you're buying, what you're thinking, when your birthday is, who you voted for, and what you're doing this weekend. And it had all better be awesome. Life has always been competitive; now it's just competitive under the guise of online "friendship." It sometimes feels like you're receiving that vomit-inducing end-of-the-year holiday "update" letter except you're receiving it every day of your life.

I quit Facebook three months ago and haven't thought about it since.

Lest this become the typical "old guy ranting about Facebook" essay, the point here is we are our own American idols, and much of what we do, we do under the guise of self-sufficiency. We want people to know that we're okay. We want them to know that our job is awesome, our weekend was absolutely unforgettable, we just ate at this week's Restaurant of the Year, and that we're more attractive than ever. Besides being mostly patently untrue, this is an insidious, culturally encouraged form of idolatry to which I have spent many years succumbing. We talk about relying solely on Christ for our joy and peace, but the message we're sending online is anything but.

Losing the Great American Hero

I spent last night in the Detroit airport after receiving a call from my agent that the highest of high-profile college athletes of our generation requested my presence in Mobile, Alabama, at the Under Armour Senior Bowl this morning. This particular college hero is the kind of lantern-jawed, intentionally stubbled, dreamy-eyed Great American Mega-Hero after whom babies are named in certain parts of the Southeastern Conference where college football is played at the highest level. I shouldn't tell you his name for career-elongating (mine) purposes, because if I were to make fun of this All-American Hero, I might never work in this town (publishing, Christian) again. I'm not going to tell you.

It's [name omitted by publisher].

Hero's family had been in semifrequent communiqué with my agent (note: I still like saying "my agent") about a ghostwritten "autobiography"—the kind that would feature his stubbly, lantern-jaw on the cover and be filled with approximately 201 pages of anecdote, pith, and inspiration. The kind of book about which ninth-grade sports-playing males across the country might say, "It's my favorite book ever." I would never write this kind of book in real life, but let's be totally honest here: I need the money, and this kid is the hottest selling thing imaginable right now.

I'm in the lobby of the Under Armour Senior Bowl hotel in Mobile, and the place is filled, pillar to post, with people of all ages wearing American Hero's college jersey. They're everywhere. Out the picturesque picture window in front of the hotel is a sidewalk, also jammed with people wearing American Hero's jersey. Rumor has it (via the agent) that he was offered a $1 million book contract the minute after his college career expired, for a book with no proposal and no coauthor attached. I am here under the auspices that I might be that coauthor. Hero's parents have been using my agency to evaluate all of the potential book deals that are coming their way. That bodes well for me.

I received the agent call at 7:30 p.m., while I was enjoying a late dinner of Chinese food with my family. I had an hour to procure a ticket, pack a bag ("arty-casual"—my wife's words), and prepare a pitch for American Hero and his family, all of whom I'm supposed to be meeting here in the lobby. My wife kissed me as I left the house, full of dreams that a potential seven-figure book deal can kick-start. "You gotta go down there and take your shot," she said, parroting the kind of sports-vernacular she'd heard me use in the past. She was convinced that American Hero's family would love me and offer me the deal.

Back in the lobby I am briefly mobbed when, for a minute, some prepubescent female fans (see: jersey) and their mother think that I am American Hero's brother. I produce my notebook and shoulder bag as, sort of, *proof* that I'm working and not just in Mobile eating comped meals and being a part of an entourage.

I'm motioned toward the elevator where we will ride to the top floor and enter a hospitality suite that looks like it was designed to emulate the hospitality suite in the movie *Jerry Maguire*. We're joined in the elevator by a middle-aged lady from Memphis who is determined to tell us just how much American Hero has meant to her and her brothers, cousins, and children. She's wearing an officially licensed University of (Omitted) hoodie.

I'm killing it. Personality plus, given the fact that I only slept a few hours.

It's understood that I will loll amicably in the suite by myself for the remainder of the afternoon, until American Hero himself emerges from practice. He is having a rough week. He has strep throat and is also having trouble playing in a pro-style offense where he has to receive a snap from center rather than in a "shotgun" formation.

Finally Hero emerges through the front door and the entire suite seems to re-energize with his presence. He is chewing gum. He looks just like he does on television and, despite the strep, looks remarkably chipper. He has a couple of those Lance Armstrong-ish bracelets around his wrist, except that they have Bible verses on them. We banter the easy banter of football players. We even toss the ball back and forth a couple times (seriously, we do). He is visited by a not-unattractive co-ed who just a few months ago was burned severely in a bonfire and wanted more than anything to meet American Hero. They meet and their conversation isn't really even that awkward, given the circumstances. Given his outrageous comic-book fame, I expect American Hero to be way more of a jerk.

Hero's people ask me all kinds of questions about my background, my faith, my football career, and my writing. I answer all of them semi-charmingly, I think, but one can never tell. There is even a joke made about how American Hero had lots of help writing all of his college papers while at the University of (Wherever). Chuckles all around. We'll celebrate when the ink is on the paper, is what I always tell my wife. I'm bleary-eyed but flying high on the potential when I shake hands with a rep from Hero's entourage at the end of the night. "We'll be in touch within the week," he says. "If this thing is gonna happen, it's gonna happen fast."

I book a hotel room and open my laptop, Jerry Maguire–style. I hammer out a book proposal and most of the first chapter that night. For what it is, which is a fawning jock autobiography, I think it's kind of amazing.

"Within the week" turns into six months. I haven't heard a thing from Hero or his family. I see him on television occasionally. I see that he has signed what is sure to be a decently lucrative endorsement deal. I see him celebrating with his family after being drafted (controversially) in the first round of the NFL draft. His family is shown on ESPN celebrating in their already richly appointed suburban McMansion, and they're all wearing matching colored shirts. He dons a team cap and says something about it being a blessing and a dream come true.

I'm in Florida speaking at a conference when I learn that Hero might hire a certain popular Christian woman to coauthor his book. She has thus far specialized in the kinds of Christian romance novels that have a doe-eyed frontier girl on the cover, with a broad-shouldered, shy-but-has-a-heart-of-gold blacksmith (or clergyman, or schoolmaster) soft-focused in the background. She writes those kinds of books. I can't imagine her writing a football book. (Would it sound like this? "[Name Omitted's] barrel-chest heaved as he settled in under center, his hazel eyes glistening . . .") So I don't abandon all hope. It's weird to me that Hero and I have been in the same room together and may be seven-figure business partners at some point soon, but I'm getting all my information about him from the television.

I've also been told by my agent that it's a distinct possibility that nobody from Hero's camp has actually read any of the material I've submitted.

I need the money (desperately), but I'm secretly terrified to write this book, mostly because of how boring American Hero's story actually is, when you think about it. I mean sure, he's won national titles, played on national television nearly every weekend, and even circumcised a few impoverished, wide-eyed kids on his highly publicized missions trips. But he's never actually *lost* anything. He barely lost a game in college. He's never had a serious injury. His parents are still married and affluent. His siblings, for the most part, are also lantern-jawed and successful in other walks of life. He always says the right thing. Always.

This, of course, makes him almost epically boring.

Finally, a few weeks before the NFL draft, I email American Hero's camp to let them know that I'll be in Nashville, just a few blocks away from where Hero is training for the draft. They email back immediately: *We're not doing the book.*

The book was released, to great fanfare, less than a year later.

A Long Aside About What I Just Wrote

My editor, God bless him, is concerned about the section above, because he's concerned about my not looking "mature and sympathetic." I appreciate him for this. He expresses concern partly because it's his job to look out for people like me (loose cannons—who make his books interesting but who also cause him to lose sleep), and partly, I'm sure, because he's covering his own back. Still, I struggle with the fact that I'm *not* always mature and sympathetic. Sometimes I'm the bad guy (as I may well have been above), sometimes I'm the jealous guy, sometimes I'm the bitter guy (see above), and sometimes (by the grace of God) I manage to make the right decision. But as the jealous, bitter guy who often does wrong things, I run to the cross, repent, and feel forgiveness for those things.

Still, I think as a memoirist it's important to be honest and not fabricate a version of myself that everybody will be more comfortable with. So for the record, if you love Great American Hero, send your Christian hate mail to *me* and not my publisher. Actually, don't send hate mail to anybody, because what happened with Hero (Christians hurting other Christians) is just an example of how life in a fallen, sinful world works. It's an example of why we all need a Savior. Also, it will all make more sense in a few chapters, when I finally start to look like less of a jerk.

I never thought I could say that I relate a lot to Madonna, but I can really associate with the quote I used to open the chapter: "I have an iron will, and all of my will has always been to conquer some horrible feeling of inadequacy. . . . My drive in life is from this horrible fear of being mediocre." I have the same horrible fear (mediocrity), and have had, at times, the same iron will to conquer and make things happen. In America, we laud this attitude. As a young athlete I was encouraged to feel this way, and to feel that if I wasn't trying to conquer something, indeed something was wrong with me.

The only problem with this perspective, for the Christian, is that it's not only wildly unbiblical, it also negates the possibility of our ever being satisfied or ever giving God glory. The fact is that even if I'd been able to adopt Anastasia, and even if I'd landed the lucrative book deal with Great American Hero, it wouldn't have been enough. I would have found something else to need and then try to conquer.

Losing the Great American Book Deal

I would have never assented to it intellectually, but money had become my practical God. I confess that, and ask forgiveness for it. It was so insidious and subtle. I was never on the cover of *Forbes*. I never wanted to be. My cars were modest. I never had a boat. But the acquisition and saving of money—through speaking gigs, new book deals, etc.—was the thing in which I was putting my trust and faith. Ultimately, like all other idols, it disappointed me. It paled in comparison to communion with Christ.

I'd made this an idol because, sadly, my years as an evangelical had taught me that you really *can* buy most people's respect. I had overemphasized becoming a provider for my family. I didn't just want to provide. I wanted to be idolized by my family and by others. I wanted to be impressive to them and to others. Not surprisingly, God came after me, for which I am thankful beyond words. More on that later.

Around the same time that I was losing out on the project with American Hero, I had a handshake agreement with another Christian publisher to write a series of books on Christian manhood. "We want you to be the Christian manhood voice of your generation," they said with stars in their eyes, over breakfast at a swanky Chicago breakfast place called Yolk (or Egg or something)—the kind of place with art-deco furniture and exposed ductwork, where a regular omelet costs thirteen bucks because the girl who brought it to you is studying to be a model. "We've just gotta dot the i's and cross the t's," they explained. Handshakes. Smiles.

It was around this time that it was occurring to me that there were a lot of people in Christian publishing not worrying about their next paycheck. As I walked through said publisher's office, I noticed lots of people in khakis and golf shirts, occupying cubicles on a full-time, health-insurance-included basis. I, in the meantime, was spending entire nights in the fetal position on the floor, wondering how we were going to pay our mortgage on the house we had reached for. This is the lot in life for the freelance author. But still, I reasoned that if God had taken away my ability to have children biologically and my daughter via the adoption, He should at least be hooking me up professionally. What I didn't realize (at the time) was that Christian publishing was seriously messing with my ability to be a Christian.

But God, in His infinite wisdom, was using the circumstance to bring me to a place of total and complete brokenness and contrition before Him. But first He had to show me my bitter heart of stone, and begin to replace it with a heart of flesh. The process was the most painful yet redemptive thing I've ever experienced. More on that later.

As it turns out, in publishing, dotting the i's and crossing the t's can pretty much take forever. To start with, it seems like editors are only in the office about three days per year. Conferences are plentiful. Returned phone calls are few.

"We're gonna need to do some work with a focus group (see: phrases that mean your project is about to get killed)," the editor explained, saying that they "needed some clarity on the project." He wanted me to compile a group of young men off of which to bounce ideas about a series of books for young men. The words *focus group* should always elicit an eye roll. It's industry code for "I don't have the courage to make this decision on my own so I'm going to pawn it off on several other people who I can then blame when things inevitably get weird or disappointing." Everything in publishing is done by committee—everything from book acquisitions to deciding where to eat for lunch. It's so that at the end of the day, there's nobody to blame (besides the author).

It was in this spirit that the focus group finally convened, manned by a couple of pastor friends, a few of my college students, and a couple of guys I'd never seen in my life. There were donuts. There was a good deal of scribbling done on a whiteboard. All of this was as convivial as a focus group can be on a drab, February day in Michigan. I allowed myself to feel hopeful again.

A month later I received a voice mail letting me know that the project was officially dead. I had lost two book deals in the span of a few weeks, bills were mounting, and where was God in this? Further, I had been disappointed by professional Christians at every turn, which I have to admit is harder than being disappointed by regular people (which happens often in publishing as well).

My questions were practical as well as theological: Does knowing God make any difference in my life, as well as in the lives of the believers who are (I felt) wronging me? And more important, can I trust a God who would not allow me to have biological children, allow my adoption to fall through, allow me to be disappointed by Christian colleagues, and allow me to miserably fail financially?

I was the opposite of self-sufficient. I was self-insufficient.

How Church Helps in the Darkness

I started this chapter by writing about some of the ways that church doesn't necessarily help in our darkest hours. I'm going to end by writing about how it can.

In the next chapter I'll write about how there is truly nothing on earth that can touch the magnitude of the freedom that comes from redemption and forgiveness in Christ. My mission, as I see it, is to abide in Him day by day, going to Him for forgiveness of my many sins, and sharing the hope of salvation with others.

I'm helped by a church that encourages me in the following areas:

1. Bold, consistent, expositional preaching of the Word of God—the kind of preaching that often convicts its hearers of sin and leads to repentance.
2. Encouragement to repent and turn away from any known sins.
3. An equally consistent message that my only hope in this life or the next is my trust in the gospel of Jesus Christ.
4. A commitment to giving thanks and praise to a God who forgives us of our sins.

Don't get me wrong, our church does more than that—we support missionaries, we do outreach activities like Christianity Explored, and we support people in need both inside our congregation and outside. But at its essence, I think our church's "mission" (if you will) is represented in the above four points.

That doesn't mean they always get it right. That doesn't mean everybody in the lobby always has a helpful word to say (far from it). But my role isn't to wallow in despondency (more on the not wallowing later) or my church's imperfections. My church's job is to help me fight despondency, and to battle the Enemy's chief lie: that God cannot be trusted to meet my needs or satisfy me.

4

Personal Jesus

The Joyless Pursuit of Creating God in Our Own Image

RONNIE MARTIN

For me, it all started in 1981 at the Canyon High School basketball gym in Anaheim, California. There was a band playing that night called The Lifesavers (one of the original old-school Christian bands, if the name didn't give it away), and to all good parents of the 1980s, dropping your unaccompanied eleven-year-old off was perfectly fine, as long as it was at church. Canyon High School was where we happened to be going to church that particular year, as my parents were doing a bit of church hopping at the time.

It was dark and intimidating when I walked in, save for the red and blue stage lights that hovered over the platform, creating an awe-inspiring vision of grandiosity as the lights glittered against the guitars, amps, drum kit, and microphones. I felt a strange tension and nervousness as I stared at that stage, wondering what it must feel like for the band that was getting ready to entertain us. I liked the feeling.

I crossed the gym, past all the old, scary high-schoolers, and climbed to the top of one of the bleachers in the back. All of a sudden, all the lights dropped and The Lifesavers finally made their way up to the stage and launched into what at the time I could only describe as the loudest and most gloriously terrifying display of noise my young ears had ever heard. The two hundred or so kids responded appropriately and started moving and dancing and cheering, which, for a sheltered Christian school kid, was my Beatles-at-Shea-Stadium moment. I remember being totally transfixed, sitting like a motionless mannequin until about halfway through the set, when I realized that sitting in the back bleachers wasn't going to cut it anymore. Emboldened by the G-rated display of anarchy happening right before my eyes, I dashed to the side of the gym just as the lead guitarist had exited the stage to sit out a few tunes. Since this was the early '80s, he actually looked like a cross between Brian Setzer from the Stray Cats and the lead singer of Spandau Ballet. To me, he looked larger than life, and it was at that moment that I discovered my calling in life: to be him. I couldn't believe my luck as I boldly stood there next to him, wondering why throngs of manic teenage admirers weren't clamoring to be in my position. Then it happened. He looked over at me. He nodded. My heart raced. I now had a story to tell my friends the next day. More than that, I knew what I wanted my story to be in the future.

Everything Counts

The Christian music industry is a small place. Sure, it's bigger now than it's ever been, but most of the people involved in it kind of know the same people, play the same venues, and complain about it all the same. But back in 1991 it was even smaller, and that's when I came into contact with that guitar player who had nodded at me from the concert at Canyon High School ten years prior. By this time, he had cemented his reputation as a legendary figure in the ever-expanding world of Christian alternative music and was now a respected label owner. Better yet, he had acquired a copy of a demo tape I had just recorded. Better still, I had just gotten a call from a rep at his label saying they wanted to offer me a recording contract. There are certain twists of irony in life that have no explanations, and I'd probably believe this was one of those, except that I'm a Calvinist and I believe it's dumb to believe in dumb luck. What happened next was that I got my wish. A contract was signed. I had achieved the first step of a dream that had been conceived over a decade earlier. What I didn't know was how this tiny spark of opportunity would grow into a fire of self-consumption that God would have to painfully extinguish twenty years later as He prepared me for ministry.

I was an eleven-year-old kid at a Christian rock show. I could've never predicted that the seeds of pride sown into my heart that night would grow into a dark, excruciating struggle that would test the very faith I proclaimed through my art.

Shake the Disease

I don't remember ever being taught about my identity in Christ growing up as a church youth group kid who said all the right things, made all the right moves, and thought *rebellion* was a word that could only be applied to other kids who cussed a lot and probably went all the way with their girlfriends. In the controlled environment of stuffy, self-righteous youth culture, there was *us* and there was *them*. Some of *them* actually came to youth group, and they were the ones who most of the girls liked and all the other guys hated because all the girls liked them and not us. What I do remember is that I had a relationship with Christ that was based more on my fear of not performing well than a godly fear and love for a Savior who had already completed the performance for me. Because of that, I had become the functioning version of a Christian trapeze artist, taking blind leaps of self-sacrifice through the air, hoping the bar would swing back just in time for me to grab it and go for another one. I had been taught the verse about obedience being better than sacrifice, but nobody ever told me that there was this thing called grace that transformed our acts of obedience into offerings of joy. Instead, I felt compelled to draw up another checklist for Jesus, hoping He would reward my noble yet frustrating efforts. By the time I signed the contract from the record label, I was done with blind leaps and tedious checklists, but not for the reasons I should've been.

The first few years in the music scene were miserably painful to both my ego and my bank account. I had introduced a new style of European-influenced electronic music into the Christian industry, and it had most definitely not propelled me into superstardom. Although I had acquired a devout—if not overly large—group of fans, the widespread acclaim that I had dreamed about a decade earlier at that Lifesavers' show had not been attained on any level. Although depressed and consumed with equal measures of doubt and arrogance, I pressed on as hard as I knew how, as there was no way that God or anyone else in this world was going to deprive me of what I thought was rightfully mine. The ego had launched and there was no landing in sight.

The tricky thing about the Christian music scene is that it operates like a para-church ministry, meaning it's this strange organism that exists alongside the church without actually being in it. Bands typically spring from youth groups, get signed to labels, and hit the road playing churches or church-sponsored events. Like a para church, a lot of the support actually comes from church kids spending their parents' money on music that's safe for the church. Unlike a para church, it's questionable that what most artists are doing could rightfully be called "ministry." Now, I know that last comment will get some push back, and I'm not saying there aren't artists out there with legitimate ministries, it's just that it's probably rare to find ones that truly function this way. A lot of Christian artists may feel like they're doing ministry, but in reality they're simply sharing stages with pastors who are paying them out of the ministry they're already doing. Okay, I went there.

I had people telling me all day long and twice on Sunday how great it was that I had such a thriving "music ministry" and how wonderful it must feel that the Lord was using me to influence people the way I was. Now, I knew that I was influencing people, but I had grown way more interested in how people were influencing me than the other way around. My identity was so tied up in my persona as an artist that the idea that it also doubled as something I was "doing for God" simply gave me the justification necessary to continue down my well-trodden path of self-indulgence. Had I stopped lying to myself for even a minute, I would've been faced with this sobering truth: My heart had grown far from God as it swelled up in glory for me.

World Full of Nothing

Sin that goes undealt-with in our life doesn't just magically lessen with age. In fact, it does the opposite—it compounds with age and becomes responsible for stripping away the very thing we were given when Christ saved us, and that's joy. At the root of darkness, doubt, and the struggle to believe lies a vacancy of joy in our hearts, and that's because joy can't share space with anything that threatens to destroy it. The reality is that God blesses us with joy so that regardless of the amount of material blessings we receive in this life, our hunger and thirst for Him is never replaced by those material things. When a Christian is truly immersed in the pursuit of the gospel, those material blessings function as occasions for thankfulness.

Joy happens as the result of being fulfilled by one person, and that's Jesus.

I had come to a point where I was getting no fulfillment from being in Christ. My only sense of fulfillment was from the accomplishments I was trying to earn from the blessings of Christ, which had turned into burdens because they had become ultimate things. I had taken a small talent, a skill I had been given for writing songs and programming synthesizers (of all things), and turned it into a graven image. Instead of glorifying God for the small talents He had graciously given me, I instead worshiped what came as the result of those talents. Worse still, my life pursuit had become doing everything I could so others might worship my talent. The result? Anger, resentment, pride, arrogance, and a lifestyle that kept me pursuing self-worship like a drug addict searches maniacally for his next fix. Did I ever sense an imbalance? I think I did, but remember, I was also doing "ministry," so whenever those nagging thoughts came bubbling to the surface, courtesy of the Holy Spirit, I simply gave myself another shot of "spiritual" self-accomplishment and carried on.

If this was a typical *Behind the Music* story, I'd tell you that I ended up sliding into a life of sex, drug abuse, alcohol overconsumption, and the worse kind of debauchery and addiction until miraculously God came into my life and delivered me from evil. (If you're unfamiliar with *Behind the Music*, I'll describe it in the next section.) But none of those things happened. There was no substance abuse, and I remained faithful to my wife through my entire life on the road. In fact, my story is really no different from anyone else who started loving something more than God, other than by the grace of God I was spared some of the earth-shattering side effects. We don't need sensational stories with dramatic endings to exist for despondency and despair to become the inevitable conclusions of our life. But some people do. For some of them, God uses a more severe mercy. In a letter to a friend who was suffering from the death of his wife, C. S. Lewis wrote, "One way or another the thing had to die. Perpetual springtime is not allowed. You were not cutting the wood of life according to the grain. There are various possible ways in which it could have died tho' both parties went on living. You have been treated with a severe mercy."[1]

Pleasure Little Treasure

I used to love the show *Behind the Music* on VH1. It was an hour-long program that featured the true-life tragedies and triumphs behind mega-selling artist/musicians. There were typically three parts. First would be the story of how they got started and all the struggles they experienced working in the trenches before they finally got their big break. Next, they'd flash to the golden age of their career after they had become household names and the world was at their feet. Finally, they'd come back from a commercial, the music would take

1. Walter Hooper, ed., *The Collected Letters of C. S. Lewis, Volume 3* (New York: Harper Collins, 2007), 606.

a dark turn, and you'd see how it all came crashing down through death, drugs, alcohol, and/or changing trends. It would always wind down on a more hopeful note, providing the audience with a snapshot of the rejuvenated band or artist trying to desperately claw their way back into the limelight with the help of family, friends, and Dr. Drew. Almost every episode was the same.

The story of King Nebuchadnezzar was one of the originals!

An interesting guy with a weird name, Nebuchadnezzar was an Assyrian king during Israel's exile in the Old Testament. He occasionally hung out with a God-fearing Hebrew guy named Daniel who was pretty smart and could interpret dreams. Neb became a believer, but he still struggled heavily with pride. One of the things we can count on God to do in the life of a believer is to get really severe with our sins. Things like anger, pride, and arrogance don't go unchecked in God's economy forever. As a loving Father, God disciplines us and takes things away that hinder our growth, maturity, and love for Him. Isaiah 2:11 tells us that "The haughty looks of man shall be brought low, and the lofty pride of men shall be humbled, and the LORD alone will be exalted in that day." The sin of pride is the insatiable desire to see ourselves exalted above everything and everyone else, including God. Although most of us would say we stop before the God part, consider what the true aim of our pride was from the beginning: to be like God. It starts the second we're conceived in sin, takes root the first time we utter the word *mine*, and spreads like a cancer until Christ reaches down and miraculously heals what is an otherwise incurable disease.

The story of Nebuchadnezzar is a graphic example of what happens when our pride reaches epic proportions. In God's grace, he was given a warning from his buddy Daniel. There was a moment when Nebuchadnezzar could have believed

God's warning, repented, and received reconciliation, but he didn't. His pride distorted the clarity of his mind, heart, and vision. It always does. Here's what happened:

> All this came upon King Nebuchadnezzar. At the end of twelve months he was walking on the roof of the royal palace of Babylon, and the king answered and said, "Is not this great Babylon, which I have built by my mighty power as a royal residence and for the glory of my majesty?" While the words were still in the king's mouth, there fell a voice from heaven, "O King Nebuchadnezzar, to you it is spoken: The kingdom has departed from you, and you shall be driven from among men, and your dwelling shall be with the beasts of the field. And you shall be made to eat grass like an ox, and seven periods of time shall pass over you, until you know that the Most High rules the kingdom of men and gives it to whom he will." Immediately the word was fulfilled against Nebuchadnezzar. He was driven from among men and ate grass like an ox, and his body was wet with the dew of heaven till his hair grew as long as eagles' feathers, and his nails were like birds' claws.
>
> At the end of the days I, Nebuchadnezzar, lifted my eyes to heaven, and my reason returned to me, and I blessed the Most High, and praised and honored him who lives forever,
>
>> for his dominion is an everlasting dominion,
>>> and his kingdom endures from generation to generation;
>> all the inhabitants of the earth are accounted as nothing,
>>> and he does according to his will among the host of heaven
>> and among the inhabitants of the earth;
>> and none can stay his hand
>>> or say to him, "What have you done?"
>
> At the same time my reason returned to me, and for the glory of my kingdom, my majesty and splendor returned

to me. My counselors and my lords sought me, and I was established in my kingdom, and still more greatness was added to me. Now I, Nebuchadnezzar, praise and extol and honor the King of heaven, for all his works are right and his ways are just; and those who walk in pride he is able to humble.

Daniel 4:28–37

Okay, that's dramatic. But what an illustration of the lengths that God will go to jealously guard both His glory and our joy. Most of us will probably never experience anything as over-the-top as Nebuchadnezzar did, but we can experience the way he was humbled before his people and the Lord. That's a good thing, by the way.

What can we learn from the darkness of Nebuchadnezzar's pride and idolatry? Here was someone who was taken from the heights of societal prestige, success, and power, to the absolute lowest human condition imaginable. It was the severity of God's mercy on Nebuchadnezzar that allowed him to learn of God's absolute sovereignty over all things: "Until you know that the Most High rules the kingdom of men and gives it to whom he will" (Daniel 4:32). When we think of who God is and the majesty of His power and authority over all things, we begin to understand how loving He was toward King Neb for letting him suffer through the condition He put him through. Instead of simply imagining the horror and humiliation that Neb went through (and it's good that we do), it better directs our eyes toward the loving hand of a Creator at work to restore His servant back to himself. Although it's a concept that we struggle to grasp, God had every right to destroy Nebuchadnezzar for worshiping the glory of his kingdom over the God who had appointed him to rule over it. Instead, He exposes Nebuchadnezzar. He causes him to go through temporary insanity to eventually bring him back to a sane mind who could praise, honor, and glory in "him who lives forever" (Daniel 4:34).

There's a part of my story that can relate to Nebuchadnezzar, though the outcome of mine seems trivial in comparison. At the lowly heights of my music career, I experienced what could be called temporary insanity. In exchange for the fruit of the Spirit, I was experiencing and exhibiting the rotten fruit of my self-absorption. My pride was trading the gifts of the Spirit for the sins of the flesh.

Love for fear.

Joy for anger.

Peace for chaos.

Patience for intolerance.

Kindness for mean-spiritedness.

Goodness for selfish motivations.

Faithfulness for disloyalty.

Gentleness for irritability.

Self-control for disorder.

With thankfully less drama, God brought me as close to the end of myself as I'd ever been. I say "close," because I'm certainly still someone who's overly concerned with his own well-being. But like Nebuchadnezzar, I had to lift my eyes to heaven . . . bless the Most High, and praise and honor him who lives forever (see Daniel 4:34). It was the only way to find restoration and feel whole again. I had to come to grips with a passage in James that serves as a warning siren to all believers.

But if you have bitter jealousy and selfish ambition in your hearts, do not boast and be false to the truth. This is not the wisdom that comes down from above, but is earthly, unspiritual, demonic. For where jealousy and selfish ambition exist, there will be disorder and every vile practice.

James 3:14–16

Sin creates regret. Looking back, I lost a number of precious years mired in the fog of idolatry and disillusionment. I had bought into an earthly, unspiritual, and demonic rationale that kept my mind in a perpetual state of chaos and disorder. "For all that is in the world—the desires of the flesh and the desires of the eyes and pride of life—is not from the Father but is from the world" (1 John 2:16).

I felt no peace, and I had none to give. Like Nebuchadnezzar, I needed to lift my eyes to heaven. I needed to humble myself. I needed to repent.

One's pride will bring him low, but he who is lowly in spirit will obtain honor.

Proverbs 29:23

It's through repentance that God grants us a lowly spirit. Acknowledging Him once again as the Lord of our lives is what brings reason back into it. Believing that "all his works are right and his ways are just" (Daniel 4:37) is what anchors us. It's the word *all* that tells us God makes no arbitrary movements in His universe. But what about our movements? What about the mistakes, missteps, and malfunctions that we consistently make time and time again? What about the bad decisions and bad timing that characterize our lives? What about that? They all work to accomplish what God plans to accomplish. We have no power to prevent what only God can purpose.

And none can stay his hand or say to him, "What have you done?"

Daniel 4:35

This was glorious news for Nebuchadnezzar. He got his life back. He didn't have to live like an animal anymore, shaming himself, his kingdom, and his people. He could be whole again, free from the burden of insanity that his pride had driven him to. His repentant heart brought him the honor of his kingdom back.

My counselors and my lords sought me, and I was established in my kingdom, and still more greatness was added to me.

Daniel 4:36

Enjoy the Silence

Sometimes we can't remember where it all went wrong. In the beginning I just wanted to be a songwriter. I loved songs, and there was something about the process of creating something out of nothing that intrigued me. I spent hours listening to simple, beautifully crafted pop songs and hoped that someday I would learn how to do it. In an era before Myspace, iTunes, and Bandcamp, it felt like an impossible dream that I might be afforded the opportunity for anyone to actually listen to, much less *buy* something I wrote. Eventually I was given an inch, but what I desperately wanted was a mile. It wasn't enough to simply enjoy something God had given me an interest and desire for. Instead, it birthed a hunger in me that could never be filled. My appetite had become insatiable. There was nothing that occupied my thoughts more than music. When I wasn't writing, performing, or recording, I was planning tours, designing merchandise, buying gear, corresponding with managers, meeting with my booking agent, and dialoguing with my label . . . all day, every day. And you know what? People admired me for it. They respected how hard I worked and how devoted I was to my art. What they didn't know was how self-centered, self-indulgent, self-consumed, and self-focused I was, at the expense of personal relationships and spiritual growth. I had traded my hope in Christ for a religious experience called "me."

We're all given raw materials. We're each given a portion. In reality, it's only by God's amazing grace we're given anything at all. Sadly, our base tendency is to hoard, feed on, and become gluttons with the things God has privileged us to be stewards over. Instead of praising Him for the portion He's given us, we indulge in it because we don't think God has been generous enough. We love our goods more than our God. How tragic would it be if one of our kids opened a gift we bought them but promptly ran away, never spoke to us again, and spent every waking moment caring for and obsessing over the gift instead? Imagine the confusion and horror of trying to understand why they would choose a gift over the one who gave them the gift! Our first reaction would be to find them and get rid of the gift as soon as possible, because it had ceased to be the thing we gave them. Instead of an object given out of our affection, it had become *the* object of their affection.

Anytime we love our gifts more than the Giver of gifts, we enter into a state of disharmony, dissatisfaction, and disarray, and plunge headlong into the dark side effects of those heart conditions. Because we were created by a God who is above all else, we were never meant to put anything else above Him.

It's a convicting, heartbreaking truth.

The reason we struggle with our desire for the things of God is because we've cultivated a stronger love for the things He gave us. We need to recognize, itemize, and then repent. We need to come to the place Nebuchadnezzar came to and say, "Now I, Nebuchadnezzar, praise and extol and honor the King of heaven, for all his works are right and his ways are just; and those who walk in pride he is able to humble" (Daniel 4:37).

That we would become broken before God, the One who breaks our idols and rebuilds our joy in Him.

5

I Built My Fortress

*Mistaking Failure for Humility,
and Killing Big T*

TED KLUCK

I don't play for the critics.
—Russell Hammond,
Stillwater, from
Almost Famous

Self-love became absolute master of his soul, and
the more noble and spiritual principles of his being
took wings and flew away.

—Jonathan Edwards on self-love

Everything is safe which we commit to Him. Nothing is safe which is not so committed.

—A. W. Tozer, *The Pursuit of God*

God was leading me on a journey toward complete broken-ness, but He still had a few idols left to destroy, including the praise of man. Because even if I was effectively going broke, and even if I had lost a few book deals, most people didn't know. I still had an impressive website. I still had a Facebook fan page full of interesting photos from book signings and links to upcoming speaking engagements. And I was still Big T, the life of the proverbial party.

You see, there's a fundamental difference between Ted and Big T. Ted is for the most part genuinely humble, self-effacing, and decent. Ted was the shy kid in school who sat in the back corner close to the door, drew pictures in his notebook, and was too nervous to ever say anything to anybody. Ted was afraid to go out with his friends on Friday nights for fear that his parents would be bored or disappointed without him around. Ted's idea of a good time is sitting alone in a rocking chair and listening to music.

Big T, by contrast, is hilarious, sarcastic, always has a line of banter, throws the best parties, and secretly manipulates every event or conversation in such a way that the outcome serves to make Big T feel better about Big T. Big T Googles himself. Big T reads only his five-star reviews on Amazon. Big T wishes he was (and sometimes thinks he is) The Most Interesting Man Alive from those Dos Equis beer commercials. Big T reads his blog comments over and over again. Big T can always make you laugh and feel like a million bucks in the church lobby. Big T thinks he can build his own fortress, provided he keeps the social calendar full and the good reviews rolling in.

The Descent Into Cynicism

I was in Chicago when I received the *Publishers Weekly* review for my second book, *Paper Tiger: One Athlete's Journey to the Underbelly of Pro Football*. I was proud of the book—the account of a season I spent playing in a low-rent arena football league. I had literally bled and sweated all over that book; it was my best shot at impersonating one of my literary heroes, George Plimpton.

That day in Chicago I spent the morning doing touristy things like riding the train into the city, splashing around with my kids at Millennium Park, and drastically overpaying for a bag of flavored popcorn.

It was on the train ride home that I received an email from my editor, saying something like, "Hey, at least *PW* reviewed your book. . . . Chin up." That was worrisome. I read the review, then read it over again. It was so scathing that I wondered if I had, at some point in my life, personally wronged the reviewer at *PW*. I was devastated and felt like an abject failure as a writer. Through all of this I thought I was being humbled. We often describe failure as "a humbling experience." This is the whole "At least you're building character" argument. I was devastated. When my wife asked "What's wrong?" I said "Nothing." I was lying and, of course, she knew it. I swore. I ranted. I raved. I doubted God's goodness. I stood on my own rights. I ranted about what I would do to the guy, *Goodfellas*-style, if I ever ran across him. Instead of praying and trusting God with the circumstance, I enacted the typical male "I've been disrespected" gangster-ethic that we all seem to have picked up from television and film. If I've been disrespected, somebody has to pay.

But I wasn't becoming humble; I was becoming embittered and cynical. My heart, gradually, was being hardened. I was seeing the doctrine of Total and Inherited Depravity on full display in my own heart. As Tozer writes in *The Pursuit of God,* "There is within the human heart a tough, fibrous root of fallen life whose nature it is to possess, always to possess."[1]

And sadly, I can tell you from experience that sometimes cynicism can be fun. I almost made a career out of it as a freelancer for ESPN.com Page 2 at the height of the "Sportswriters Should Always Be Bitingly Acerbic and Funny" Internet boom (see: Simmons, Bill). It was my job to expect the worst from people and make fun of everything. I did both, with great enthusiasm.

Cynicism is described accurately by author Paul Miller in *A Praying Life*: "Shattered optimism sets us up for the fall into defeated weariness and, eventually, cynicism. You'd think it would just leave us less optimistic, but as humans we don't do neutral well. We go from seeing the bright side of everything to seeing the dark side of everything. We feel betrayed by life."[2]

And when we feel betrayed by life—and God—sin usually follows. We sin because we fundamentally distrust that God's plan will be enough to bring us the happiness (or esteem or comfort) that we crave the most. So we look to the world to provide those things. And many times, from Christians, we're just implored to "sin less." We buy the forty-ninth Internet filter for our computers, or take on our fifth accountability partner. Those things, mind you, are good and helpful. But like John Piper asserts in *Future Grace*, we must replace the sin with something greater.[3]

I feel like I was living proof of Miller's definition, and what I needed (besides, let's be honest, a change in circumstances) was a change in heart. I needed to be reminded of God's

1. A. W. Tozer, *The Pursuit of God* (Christian Miracle Foundation Press, 2011) Kindle edition.
2. Paul Miller, *A Praying Life: Connecting With God in a Distracting World* (Colorado Springs: NavPress, 2009), 81.
3. John Piper, *Future Grace* (Colorado Springs: Multnomah Books, 2005), 75.

goodness and also to actively be *trusting* in the goodness of God's sovereign plan for me. Through my bitterness and cynicism, I was sinning by doubting in three specific areas: One, that God is *sovereign*. Two, that God is *working* all things for my good. And three, that God is *good*.

The Audacity of Hope: Pursued by the Hound of Heaven

For most of my thirty-five years on earth, I had intellectually assented to most of what I knew to be true about Christianity. I knew, deep down, that God was real. I knew that the Bible was the inspired Word of God. I knew that the church, despite her flaws, was the bride of Christ. I had been raised in a Christian home by parents who, though flawed, loved God and loved each other. I had never "rebelled" in the traditional sense of the word. I didn't party or chase girls in college. I didn't "go off the deep end" while I was young, resulting in chronic hand-wringing by my parents. I never got a tattoo—even the "safe, evangelical kind" that features some combination of Hebrew writing, a Jesus fish, and/or a Bible verse. As a people-pleaser by nature, it was my job to keep everyone in my life happy, and doing so meant not rebelling. But I'd never had what I would call an *experience* with God. I was jealous of people who had.

But for a week in early December 2011, the hound of heaven pursued me. It began with a Sunday sermon, and the conviction—for sins past and present—continued through the following Saturday. With each passing day I was eating and sleeping less, but it wasn't the kind of tormented insomnia where I felt abandoned by the Holy Spirit (I've had that). It was as though, like Jacob, I was battling with the Spirit through the Scriptures. I tried to flush the feeling with movies and music (my usual go-to distractors). Nothing worked. Everything reminded me of the Scriptures. God was chasing me down. As a former linebacker, I could relate to pursuit—I used to daydream about chasing down running backs and quarterbacks and crushing them. Now I was the pursue-ee. I was the one being crushed by the Spirit.

At night I sat on the floor of our walk-in closet (this is, after all, suburban torment), surrounded by jeans, button-down shirts, and jerseys, reading the Psalms. It was the detritus of my life, and proof of the kinds of fortresses I'd tried to build for myself. Designer jeans. Hipster canvas shoes. My college and arena football jerseys. That seems like a million years ago.

I was becoming convicted, finally, that I needed to confess sin to God, my church, and the people I'd hurt. I was afraid, but it wasn't all lonely, hopeless fear. I had felt lonely and hopeless before—in fact for much of my thirties—but this was different. Confession takes courage, but God gives hope, peace, and courage. For the first time in my life I understood what people meant when they said things like, "It wasn't me, it was God." I had, again, intellectually assented to the idea of "giving God the glory" for things, but until now I had no practical experience with it.

I wanted the kind of communion with God that A. W. Tozer wrote about in *The Pursuit of God*: "But let him come defenseless before the Lord and he will have as his defender no less than God himself. Let the inquiring Christian trample underfoot every slippery trick of his deceitful heart and insist upon frank and open relations with the Lord."[4]

These "frank and open relations," for me, meant cultivating an ability to give and receive grace. Since I'd felt the full flush of God's grace—my soul felt clean and white again—I was able to *give* grace. My approach to my wife and my kids

4. Tozer, Kindle edition.

began to change. My historically short fuse began to lengthen. I was looking for ways to give grace, because grace was being poured onto me in abundance.

I was beginning to kill Big T, in hopes of replacing him with Ted. The Ted who was his father's son, and who was a child of God.

The Link Between Confession and Joy

In *The Joy of Calvinism*, author Greg Forster writes, "The Bible commands us to rejoice all the time. God says that if there is even a tiny fraction of a split second when we're not rejoicing, that's disobedience."[5]

By the grace of God, I was being made aware of some long-undealt-with areas of sin in my own life including (but definitely not limited to) arrogance, pride, cynicism and a kind of pervasive lack of humility. Not the kind of pervasive lack of humility that wears sunglasses in the building, demands the best of everything, and routinely big-times people. Not that kind at all. In fact, I was the antithesis of that. I was the kind of un-humble person who *lived* for the praise of others (and therefore used people *for* praise), and who would quietly seethe when I felt others were receiving credit or success that I thought I deserved more. In America we sometimes call that competitiveness, but in reality it's just sin (jealousy, envy), and it makes a person (read: me) the worst kind of jerk at times. Slowly realizing that has been like having my skin scraped away with sandpaper. It's been painful and humbling. I think previously I had confused failure with humility—that is, when something would go wrong, as it often did, I would confuse it with "becoming more humble." I apologize for that, and I

5. Greg Forster, *The Joy of Calvinism: Knowing God's Personal, Unconditional, Irresistible, Unbreakable Love* (Wheaton, IL: Crossway, 2012) 1.

particularly apologize for how that attitude/cynicism found its way into some of my writing.

A Blueprint for Confession

King David, described as "a man after God's own heart," gives us a blueprint for humble, passionate, honest, and broken confession in Psalm 51. Like Big T (to some degree—and yes, I'm now referring to my nickname in the third person . . . blame it on all the NBA basketball I watch), David's greatest strengths were his greatest weaknesses. He was good-looking, driven, charismatic, and had the ability to make things happen. People were drawn to him because of his power. It was this power that plunged David into sexual sin with Bathsheba (what a great temptress name) and drove him to send her husband, Uriah, to the battlefield to be killed.

Sin is insidious that way. It dulls and hardens our heart and slowly kills our conscience. The first thing David did, no doubt, was to justify his actions. Perhaps he thought, *I work hard, I deserve this,* or *I'm the king and these are just my executive privileges.* Perhaps, when he was sending Uriah into battle he thought, *He's a soldier anyway, this is his job. I'm not committing murder.* David, like me, had a truckload of people patting him on the back and lining up to spend time with him. He had bought into his own hype, and it had turned the volume down on his conscience.

Psalm 51 is a blueprint for confession, but it's not a self-flagellating confession. It's the kind of confession that contends, hard, for joy. David, like Jacob, is wrestling with the Spirit and refusing to let go until he receives his blessing.

> Have mercy on me, O God,
> according to your steadfast love;

according to your abundant mercy
blot out my transgressions.

v. 1

This is David's cry for forgiveness and an acknowledgement of God's greatness. Through God's conviction of David, he never lost sight of the immutable truth of God's essential *goodness*. And like all good writers, he goes to lengths to *quantify* the goodness, highlighting God's mercy, His unfailing love, and His compassion. When I was on the floor in the walk-in closet, this is the passage I read more than any other. I wanted to believe, like David, and God *allowed* me to feel His goodness in abundance.

"This is a fierce, almost desperate clinging to God's mercy," writes James Montgomery Boice in his *Expositional Commentary on the Psalms*. "This is profound because as many commentators have pointed out, mercy is the sole basis of any approach to God by sinners."[6]

As a football player and boxer, I'm well acquainted with ferocity and fierceness. It was the one quality, above all others, by which we were measured. Being described as *fierce* was a compliment of the highest order. I'm also well acquainted with evangelical publishing's semi-awkward relationship with manhood. We've been taught that manhood is "an adventure" (eye roll). We go to elaborate lengths to plan elaborate "manhood rituals" (the giving of swords and other such ridiculousness) to our sons when they turn a certain age. The fact of the matter is that life isn't much of an adventure most of the time. It's more like a marathon. A grind.

Perhaps the fiercest, most manly thing we can do is confess sin, experience God's grace, and contend for our faith like

6. James M. Boice, *Psalms: An Expositional Commentary, Volume 2* (Grand Rapids, MI: Baker Publishing, 2005), 425

David does in this passage. This has nothing to do with what we do for a living, whether we relax with a cigar, or if we carve things out of wood or run around in the forest. There's nothing ridiculous or contrived about it. This is manhood. Let's start being men. The women in our lives will appreciate it. A pastor friend once told me, "Confession and repentance is where the power of Christianity is." That's wisdom that, of course, applies to both men and women.

> Wash me thoroughly from my iniquity,
> and cleanse me from my sin!
> For I know my transgressions,
> and my sin is ever before me.
>
> vv. 2–3

These two verses offer an articulate understanding of personal brokenness. David feels dirty because of what he's done, and he wants to be clean. Anyone who's sinned in a big way knows that the sin is "always before" them. Walking, driving, talking on the phone, working out, and watching TV . . . it's always there. David wants freedom from his transgressions.

Weirdly, in my own life, I've never heard anybody articulate this feeling better than former heavyweight champion Mike Tyson, speaking at a post-fight press conference in Washington, D.C. Both of his eyes were swollen and split open by cuts. I wrote about this in my first book, *Facing Tyson: Fifteen Fighters, Fifteen Stories*. Tyson had sinned in nearly every way possible and experienced nearly everything the world had to offer financially, chemically, and sexually, and found it all to be utterly empty and lacking. "I just want to give something back," he said that night. "I've lived my whole life for myself up to now."[7] This, I thought at the time (2005,

---

7. Ted Kluck, *Facing Tyson: Fifteen Fighters, Fifteen Stories* (Guilford, CT: The Lyons Press, 2006), 16.

after his last fight with Kevin McBride), must be the epitome of hopelessness. He knew he had done bad things, and that night at least, he expressed a desire to do good things to atone for the bad things. From my Christian perspective, I knew this wouldn't ultimately work for him. It made me even sadder.

> Against you, you only, have I sinned
> and done what is evil in your sight,
> so that you may be justified in your words
> and blameless in your judgment.
>
> v. 4

This section is David's acknowledgment that in addition to sinning against Uriah and Bathsheba, he sinned first and foremost against God. Commentators are a little divided on this one. Some say, "Why doesn't David explicitly state that he also sinned against Uriah, Bathsheba, and the nation he was leading?" An honest and understandable question, for sure. According to Boice, "First, sin, by its very definition is against God, since it's only by God's law that sin is defined. A wrong done to our neighbor is a sin against humanity."[8]

David also acknowledges the appropriateness of God's judgment. He's not asking that his circumstances and consequences, necessarily, be changed. This is a picture of God we don't see much in our culture. We want God to be our cosmic drinking buddy—the guy who laughs at all our jokes and agrees with everything we're doing and thinking. We like to conveniently forget that He's a righteous judge and that this facet of God is actually a great comfort. *All* sins will eventually be paid for, either by Christ on the cross or in hell for all eternity. I realize that it makes me sound patently uncool and "fundie" to type that, but scripturally I just can't find any way around it. Nor do I want to, necessarily.

8. Boice, 427.

Behold, I was brought forth in iniquity,
and in sin did my mother conceive me.

v. 5

See: Inherited and total depravity . . . the sinful state of mankind, irreparable were it not for the Lamb of God.

Behold, you delight in truth in the inward being,
and you teach me wisdom in the secret heart.
Purge me with hyssop, and I shall be clean;
wash me, and I shall be whiter than snow.
Let me hear joy and gladness;
let the bones that you have broken rejoice.

vv. 6–8

This is David's acknowledgement that God can bring joy even in the midst of suffering. David is feeling the weight of his sin—probably on a practical consequence level as well as a "conscience" level. He feels crushed by what he's done. Notice that he doesn't ask God to restore him to a place of greatness. He simply wants joy and gladness. He wants the presence of God, and he's not afraid to ask for some relief from the pain. Notice, too, that he acknowledges God as the one who has crushed his bones. Interesting.

Hide your face from my sins
and blot out all my iniquities.
Create in me a clean heart, O God,
and renew a right spirit within me.

vv. 9–10

David desires a pure heart and a steadfast spirit, above all. Until I had a profound experience with the Holy Spirit, I couldn't say, with all certainty, that I wanted this above all. I pray that God would keep this desire in front of me.

Cast me not away from your presence
and take not your Holy Spirit from me.

v. 11

David, who has had experiences with God, wants to *keep* having experiences with God. He knows that as circumstances are changing—though outwardly he's wasting away—what he wants above all is to be in God's presence. He knows that the worst thing imaginable would be for the Lord to give him over to his sins, and to harden his heart irreparably. If this isn't terrifying to us, it should be. Again, as comfortable, American Christians, we don't like to be terrified. But a fear of a hard heart and a fear of God's judgment are exceedingly healthy. Pray that God would cultivate this.

Restore to me the joy of your salvation
and uphold me with a willing spirit.

v. 12

Joy and sustenance—this is what we all want, isn't it? Herein lies the audacity of the Gospel: that David can even think of experiencing joy after what he has done. But he doesn't just think of it or wistfully long for it; he *asks* God for it, with the full expectation that a good, merciful, and loving God will restore it to him. My two thoughts are that David has a lot of guts (but it's Gospel-motivated and saturated guts), and that this must be a pretty amazing God that he's praying to.

Then I will teach transgressors your ways,
and sinners will return to you.

v. 13

David wants to tell the story of this glorious grace, and he wants others to feel it.

Deliver me from bloodguiltiness, O God,
O God of my salvation,
and my tongue will sing aloud of your righteousness.

v. 14

David is ready to spend the rest of his life telling this glorious story of his restoration. And he does. We have David to thank for some of the most beautiful, heartfelt, passionate, and honest writing in all of Scripture. The Psalms. David felt the full weight of his sin, but also the full weight and experience of God's forgiveness and cleansing. This is the same experience that is available to us, in the face of our sins and guilt.

O Lord, open my lips,
and my mouth will declare your praise.
For you will not delight in sacrifice, or I would give it;
you will not be pleased with a burnt offering.
The sacrifices of God are a broken spirit;
a broken and contrite heart, O God, you will not
despise.

vv. 15–17

David makes a passionate argument against works-righteousness here at the end of this section. He reminds us that God does not delight in burnt offerings. He doesn't want our money or, necessarily, our impressive spiritual résumés. He wants brokenness and contrition. That, David writes, He will never despise.

And oddly, out of the brokenness and contrition, comes joy.

6

Blue Monday

Reflections on Doubt and Unbelief

RONNIE MARTIN

A true story about a family I know.

Christmas had been less than great that year for the man, his wife, and their teenage daughter. What had tradition- ally been their favorite and most celebrated time of the year had felt strained and forced, lacking the usual lightness and joy. The once glorious anticipation that would build in their hearts as December unfolded was largely absent. Though all the family traditions had been dutifully kept, the decorations carefully arranged, and the presents beautifully wrapped, something was missing.

The family had struggled trying to get acquainted with their new life in a strange town. The move had required some adjusting, since they came from a more populated area and were now trying to settle into a new way of living. Although they terribly missed all the family and friends they left behind, they felt that God had brought them to this quaint little community. They hoped it wouldn't be too long before it felt like home.

More than anything else, the man and his wife were worried about their daughter. They knew how hard it was for her to leave her friends and how afraid she was at the thought of trying to make new ones. They were proud of how brave she had been. Her father remembered her standing on the stairs at the old house as she hugged her childhood friend good-bye. He shared their tears as he watched from a distance. They promised they would see each other again. He hoped they would.

A month or two after their arrival, the daughter had already made some new friends. They seemed nice too. The man and his wife were thrilled and felt like their prayers had been answered. They thought back to the year before when their daughter had given her life to Christ and had gotten baptized at their old church. They remembered how they both cried as she read her testimony and gave thanks to God for the work He had so evidently begun in her life.

The first year went by quickly. The family had settled into a nice routine and was learning to enjoy some of the benefits that came with small town life. Everything was close, there was no traffic, people were friendly, and things moved at a much more leisurely pace. It felt like people paused to enjoy things a little bit more here than they did back home. They felt like maybe they did too.

Unfortunately, things were turning out a little different for their daughter. Some of the friendships she had made in the beginning had started to dwindle. New friends began to appear, but they were completely unlike the kind of people she normally chose to be around. Her attitude was changing too. It was hard to put a finger on it, but she was more withdrawn and cynical. When her parents would ask her questions, she would sometimes snap at them or not say anything at all. When they tried to discuss anything spiritual with her, she seemed agitated, impatient, and unwilling to open up. Instead of the time she used to spend downstairs in the kitchen with her mother or in the living room with her father, she now retreated to her bedroom, clicking away on her computer, alone.

The man and his wife had started to become sad again, like the times before she had recommitted her life to Christ. Christmas came and went. The distance was becoming intolerable. They prayed. He tried to talk to her, but she refused to say anything.

New Years came and went. School was back in session. It was a frigid day when the father met his daughter at the coffee shop. They had started meeting there once a week. She seemed unusually distracted that day and wouldn't meet his eyes when they talked. Her eyes looked dark and a little glassy as she nervously pulled a note out of her purse. She told her father that there was something she wanted to read him, and that she thought he would handle it better than her mother. The father's hands began to tremble as he steadied them around the rim of his coffee cup, all the worst possible scenarios being imagined in his head. The letter was two pages long, but the first line was the only one he heard:

"I don't believe in God anymore."

Because God is sovereign, it means that every event that unfolds in our lives is under His watchful eye and within His careful design. I don't say that flippantly, as the Bible is filled with men and women who suffered a great deal in order to understand both the joy and heartache of a God who is in complete control of things we have no ability to fathom. In a lot of ways, we learn to trust in God's foresight because of what we've learned to see in hindsight as our lives unfold with Him. Maturity in Christ is when we remember God's goodness when life is less than good. The problem with maturity is that by definition, it's something that happens over time, not instantaneously. And God takes different amounts of time to mature different people. While God took forty years to mature and humble Moses, with Paul He showed up, redirected his flight, and trained him for a new career in a new town immediately.

The daughter in the story above is on her own unique, God-directed journey, and it isn't over. Like many kids who are "born into the church," she'd been engulfed by both the blessings and curses of that her entire life. Anyone who's lived and existed in this bizarre subculture for even a short amount of time can relate to what that's like. It's riddled with clichés, rife with contradictions, and is a rude awakening to the reality that Christians are hypocrites and sinners par excellence. All of this eventually becomes exhausting, and sometimes that exhaustion can turn into bitterness and apathy if we let the culture of Christianity eclipse the Christ of Christianity. There's a rather large difference between the two. I think the girl in the story, like a lot of us, let the former infect the latter.

Doubts Even Here

If ours is an examined faith, we should be unafraid to doubt. If doubt is eventually justified, we were believing what clearly was not worth believing. But if doubt is answered, our faith has grown stronger. It knows God more certainly and it can enjoy God more deeply.

C. S. Lewis

The question of doubt is always a question of *who* over *what*. Is the *who* you are doubting a liar or a truth teller? If we believe the *who*, we never need question the *what*. I never think *what* my wife is telling me is untrue because I believe with every fiber of my being that she is someone *who* would never lie to me.

When the serpent tempted Eve in the garden, the first thing he does is call her to remember if *what* God had said to her was true. He doesn't ask her if she remembered *who* God was. That would have reminded her of God's character and that everything He said was true. So the serpent cleverly asked, "Did God actually say . . . ?" which caused her to reconstruct and rationalize God's original command to her and Adam. It caused her to call God's truthfulness into question. What the serpent challenged Eve to do was doubt the only truth she had ever known, even though the creator of truth, God, had never lied to her before. If Eve would have paused and taken those doubts and concerns back to *who* she believed God was, she might have remembered that *what* He said about not eating the fruit was a trustworthy command for her own good. Unfortunately, Eve's doubt about *who* God was led to her pride over *what* he commanded, and all of earth and creation is still reeling from the aftereffects.

How about good ol' Peter the apostle? He was no different from Eve. When Jesus asked him to take a nice little walk with Him on the Sea of Galilee, Peter lost sight of *who* he was walking with.

So Peter got out of the boat and walked on the water and came to Jesus. But when he saw the wind, he was afraid, and beginning to sink he cried out, "Lord, save me." Jesus immediately reached out his hand and took hold of him, saying to him, "O you of little faith, why did you doubt?"

Matthew 14:29–31

What happened as soon as Peter took his eyes off Jesus? He became afraid and began to sink. He started drowning. What's curious is that Jesus asks him why he doubted. Jesus had never lied to Peter before. He had a perfect track record with the guy. It made no logical sense for Peter to think that if Jesus asked him to walk with Him on that water, that he wouldn't be able to. It wasn't that Peter didn't believe in Jesus. He did. It was that he doubted *what* Jesus said because he forgot *who* Jesus was.

As It Was When It Was

There's probably not a Christian alive who hasn't read *The Chronicles of Narnia*. If you happen to be one of three or four people on earth (and I feel I'm being generous) who haven't gone through this religious rite of passage, here it is in a nutshell: It's the story of four English children—Peter, Susan, Edmund, and Lucy Pevensie—who find a magical land called Narnia that's ruled by a sovereign king named Aslan, who happens to be a lion. They eventually help Aslan overthrow the reign of the evil White Witch before becoming the high kings and queens of Narnia. Throughout the course of seven books, Lewis introduces an interesting cast of child characters (Eustace, Jill, and Polly, among others) who Aslan calls to battle against the evil forces that rise against him. Although some of the children come to Narnia as spoiled, sullen, malcontented unbelievers, Aslan transforms their hearts and they eventually become valiant men and women of honor,

98

compassion, and courage, fully devoted to the cause of Aslan and the preservation of Narnia.

A short but interesting scene unfolds in the seventh book in the series (entitled *The Last Battle*), where Lewis brings back all the characters from the previous six books to take part in the destruction of old Narnia and witness the creation of the "new Narnia." All of them except Susan Pevensie, the High Queen.

"Sir," said King Tirian, when he had greeted all these. "If I have the read the chronicle aright, there should be another. Has not your majesty two sisters? Where is Queen Susan?"

"My sister Susan," answered Peter shortly and gravely, "is no longer a friend of Narnia."

"Yes," said Eustace, "and whenever you've tried to get her to come and talk about Narnia or do anything about Narnia, she says, 'What wonderful memories you have! Fancy you're still thinking about all those funny games we used to play when we were children.'"

"Oh Susan!" said Jill. "She's interested in nothing nowadays except nylons and lipstick and invitations. She always was a jolly sight too keen on being grown up."

"Grown up, indeed," said the Lady Polly. "I wish she would grow up. She wasted all her school time wanting to be the age she is now and she'll waste all the rest of her life trying to stay that age. Her whole idea is to race on to the silliest time of one's life as quick as she can and then stop there as long as she can."

"Well, don't let's talk about that now," said Peter. "Look! Here are lovely fruit trees. Let us taste them."[1]

Anyone who's read *The Chronicles of Narnia* will tell you how shocked and saddened they were at this fateful news. Queen Susan was a solid, if slightly understated character

1. C. S. Lewis, *The Last Battle* (HarperCollins, 2009), Kindle edition, chapter 12.

that Lewis had developed fairly well in the first two books. She was marked by her bravery, her skill with a bow and arrow, and oftentimes, as necessary, peacemaker between her arguing siblings. To think that she would not gain entrance into the final manifestation of Narnia was unthinkable. So why didn't she? The answer is unbelief. At some point, Susan stopped believing that the experiences they had in Narnia had actually ever happened. If Susan had simply doubted her time in Narnia as nothing more than a game she had played with her over-imaginative brothers and sister, one look into the eyes of Aslan would have caused her memory to come back to her instantly. It wasn't that Susan doubted the existence of Narnia; it's that she didn't believe in the reality of Aslan. Let me explain.

Lewis described Aslan as the all-wise, all-knowing, and all-loving ruler of Narnia, which included his divine sovereignty over all who belonged to him both inside and outside the Narnian world. If this was true, it means that the faith of all true Narnians who believed in him would mature and grow stronger as their love for Aslan continued. Even if someone had doubts, Aslan would eventually crush those doubts by revealing himself to them and reestablishing their belief in him. Susan had at one time enjoyed the blessings that came with being High Queen of Narnia, but Susan had never had a true, genuine belief in Aslan himself. How do we know that? Because if it had been genuine, it would have still existed in the end. "They went out from us, but they were not of us; for if they had been of us, they would have continued with us. But they went out, that it might become plain that they all are not of us" (1 John 2:19).

Though Aslan may be a character in a children's fantasy novel, there are striking parallels between him and the God of the Bible. God keeps those He calls. Since He's the one who gives us the faith to believe in Him in the first place, we can be confident that He will alleviate our doubts when they start attacking our belief.

Touched by the Hand of God

And I am sure of this, that he who began a good work in you will bring it to completion at the day of Jesus Christ.

Philippians 1:6

Looking to Jesus, the founder and perfecter of our faith, who for the joy that was set before him endured the cross, despising the shame, and is seated at the right hand of the throne of God.

Hebrews 12:2

A few choice words to get our heads wrapped around: *began, completion, founder,* and *perfecter.* These are all words that point to Christ. Who He is, what He's done, and what He will continue to do. Since God is the actual creator and founder of our faith, we can be assured that He will complete this work of belief that He began in us. Doubt is what happens when we stop talking to God, stop reading His words, and start to forget the work He has actually accomplished. In some ways it's like temporary blindness. Like someone with 20/20 vision propelled into a dark room, letting the recent memory of vivid, colorful images become distant recollections and formless shadows. Where we once walked confidently in a bright, sunny world, taking in the magnificence of God's creation, we now walk in fear and darkness, unable to trust what obstacles lay in our path.

But God is not someone who keeps His children in the dark. What good father would do that? How many times have we run into our kids' bedrooms to ward off the monsters lurking under their beds and assure them that they are safe and protected? We tell them that "everything's okay" and that they should believe us when we tell them everything's okay. If our kids never believed us, and twenty years later we're still running into their rooms to ward off monsters, then there's an aspect of their development that isn't really complete. We'd probably take them to a professional to try and determine why, as adults, they still think monsters are under their bed.

The passage in Philippians reveals something similar yet far more reassuring about our heavenly Father. The progressive, sanctifying, and grace-filled life He started building in us will not be cut short. We will grow to full stature. He doesn't start things He doesn't finish. God is a completest. You know that old beat-up '72 Mustang convertible in your garage that you got "for a steal"? The one you've been meaning to finish up for the past decade but haven't even started on yet? That's not how God works.

Temporary blindness is just that. Temporary. We can trust that God will be faithful to pierce through the darkness of our doubts and continue to build and strengthen our belief in Him.

In a Lonely Place

Do you know that there are people sitting in your church who don't love Jesus? That some of these people have been attending your church for years and years? Do you know that some of these people lead ministries in your church? And that some of these people pray for others, help those less fortunate, recite Bible verses, and are people that you'd boast about to others as being model Christians? Do you know that some of these people don't know God? These are people living in a lonely place.

Church can be a strangely alluring and deceptive culture for those who come with the impression that it's something that it's not. In fact, depending on the person, church can be a great deterrent for someone coming to a saving knowledge of Jesus. How can this be, you say? Think about the surroundings of your average American, middle-class, suburban evangelical church. A beautifully landscaped campus. An amazing facility. Friendly, inviting people who greet you at the door, smile, shake your hand, give you a bulletin, and make no effort to intrude into your life whatsoever. Inside the midcentury-style sanctuary, there are comfortable seats, an explosive sound system, concert lighting display, and a band that plays songs that are energetic, uplifting, and bass heavy. The speaker is biblically smart, appropriately funny, and culturally relevant. After the service, there's a café that serves Starbucks, has great couches to relax on, and has plenty of pleasant people to mingle with and get to know better. On the wall next to the minimalist art displays is a large selection of brochures for all the different ministries the church provides and encourages you to become a part of. The list goes on.

Some qualifications. I don't think there's anything technically wrong with the picture I just described. I'm not a hymns-and-organs-only guy. I love minimalist art. I like as much new stuff as I do old stuff. I also believe that there are plenty of thriving, gospel-centered churches out there that have been blessed with all kinds of goodies who are faithfully proclaiming the gospel. But do you see how easy it would be for someone to exist in this kind of environment without ever acknowledging their sin, understanding God's holiness, or grasping God's transforming grace? Do you see how easy it would be, because it was that easy for one of the most tragic figures in all of biblical history: Mr. Judas Iscariot.

We don't typically name our kids Judas or Benedict anymore, and for good reason. These are two guys who committed a sin so egregious (betrayal, in case you missed both school and church growing up) that their names have become cultural black holes reserved for the nether regions of hell. Here's the thing about Judas: He was an insider. He was one of the twelve chosen disciples of Christ. This was a guy who spent three years on tour with Jesus, traveling from town to town, synagogue to synagogue, healing the sick, helping the homeless, feeding the hungry, and preaching the gospel to the multitudes. Moms looked up to him, kids traded bubble gum cards for his, and communities were transformed by the work Jesus had empowered him to do. This was a guy who was set to be one of the founders of the New Testament church, with his name on the marquee next to Peter, Paul, James, and John.

Only it never happened. None of it ever came to fruition. Judas never loved Jesus. He never believed. And he died a bloody, suicidal death.

What was going through Judas's mind while he was hanging out with Jesus in the flesh, we'll never know. What we can assume based on the account given is that Judas had a calloused, unregenerate heart, but his behavior was so convincing that even the disciples couldn't guess that he was the one who would betray Jesus at the Last Supper. Since he was one of the big twelve, his actions reflected the actions of those who knew Jesus. Yet he never really knew Him.

One of the greatest threats to the message of the gospel is behavioral modification. Judas was living proof of a person who can say all the right things, do all the right things, and have everyone around him believe he's righteous, when in fact his heart is far from God. Jesus described the conservative religious leaders of His day as people who "honor me with their lips, but their hearts are far from me" (Isaiah 29:13 NIV). This was Judas. This can also be the person attending your church who loves the blessings of the church without ever knowing or loving the One responsible for providing those blessings. *C'mon, Ronnie, are you putting these people on par with Judas?* Only insofar as they are deceived like Judas and may be heading to an eternity in the same hell as him. It's sobering, and it should be. Justification by faith alone is the only remedy for behavioral modification. It's only when God grants us the faith to believe that our behaviors finally become grace-filled and grace-fueled actions that mirror our love for Christ. Anything other than that adds to the atoning work of Christ on the cross, which is what He came to earth to accomplish.

True Faith

At the heart of doubt and unbelief is the unwillingness to submit and yield to Jesus Christ, the creator of the universe. The difference, though, is that doubt is a temporary condition that can lead to greater belief, while unbelief is the condition that condemns a person. George MacDonald once said, "Doubt can be a tool in God's hand wielded, in the lives of those who allow it, for the strengthening, not the destruction of faith."

To struggle with doubt is a process, and if you find yourself in the middle of that procession, I would encourage you to make sure your armor is strapped on tight and that you continue to move courageously forward in battle. A soldier is always better and more equipped to do battle after he's fought and survived a few of them. The Lord uses our doubts to give us greater assurance of His promises, and He wants us to be a people that are marked by this blessed assurance, not mired in the dense thickness of unanswered questions and disheartened conclusions. Francis Bacon said, "If a man will begin with certainties, he shall end in doubts; but if he will be content to begin with doubts, he shall end in certainties."[2]

The person who finds himself in uncertainty can certainly pray for certainty! The Lord knows our weaknesses and doubts before we even utter the words, and more than that, He loves to hear us come before Him with humble, honest confessions.

> The sacrifices of God are a broken spirit; a broken and contrite heart, O God, you will not despise.
>
> Psalm 51:17

Far from being something that we're ashamed of, we can find great encouragement in knowing that God will never reject our doubting hearts when they come before Him as broken hearts. We can take great encouragement from knowing that everyone whom God calls, He keeps, and they will persevere to the end.

> I give them eternal life, and they will never perish, and no one will snatch them out of my hand. My Father, who has given them to me, is greater than all, and no one is able to snatch them out of the Father's hand.
>
> John 10:28–29

I don't know what will happen to the daughter in the story at the beginning of the chapter, but I know that nothing will happen to her outside of God's knowledge or will. In fact,

---

2. Francis Bacon, *The Advancement of Learning* (Paul Dry Books, 2012), Kindle edition.

her doubt and unbelief were only able to exist at all because of the existence of God, who knew before the foundation of the world that those thoughts would come into existence.

Knowing that God is greater than our doubts gives us greater hope in Him.

7

My Father's Son

Praying Through Unbelief

TED KLUCK

I always wanted to be famous . . . loneliness is what I dread most.

—Freddie Roach, famous boxing trainer

The way to deeper knowledge of God is through the lonely valleys of soul poverty and abnegation of all things.

—A. W. Tozer, *The Pursuit of God*

But while he was still a long way off, his father saw him and felt compassion, and ran and embraced him and kissed him.

—Luke 15:20

I was thirty-five years old, and I had finally started
my life.

—Jerry Maguire

One of my fondest memories of childhood was an evening I
spent with my father when I was ten, watching the Penn State
Nittany Lions play the Miami Hurricanes in the Fiesta Bowl.
This was noteworthy, in part, because I was allowed to stay
up late to watch. It was important to my old-school, Mid-
western father that Penn State of the nameless vanilla jerseys,
the even-more-old-school coach, and the basically pristine
reputation beat the swaggering, pelvic-thrusting, touchdown-
dance, premeditating, mockery-of-school-making, military-
fatigue-wearing Miami Hurricanes.

We sat in a darkened TV room while my mom slept. The
television in the mind's eye of my memory flickered with
images of the Jerry Sandusky-led defense intercepting Vinny
Testaverde on what seemed like every other pass attempt.
Testaverde, it could be argued, was never the same. Penn State
won that game, we turned off the television, and all—at least
at the moment—was right with the world of sports. Some
semblance of justice had been upheld.

I didn't grow up a Penn State fan (I grew up in Indiana),
but I was one that night, and I sort of remained one in the
intervening years because of the memory of that great evening
I spent with my dad. And I sort of remained one because I
felt like Penn State, as a program, affirmed and shared some
of the same things that I valued.

Recently, of course, Penn State was in the news again
because of the darkest of dark scandals. Google the name
Jerry Sandusky for details of that scandal; I don't feel the
need to type them here. The same Sandusky who architected
those defenses is now implicated in the saddest (and most

sin-saturated) of situations. One of my closest friends is a pastor in the State College area, and what he described to me is a reaction (ex: people speaking in hushed tones, people wanting to make it go away) normally reserved for those who are grieving in the wake of a tragedy. The national media swirls in search of a reaction. The jobs of heads-of-state (in this case the venerable Joe Pa) are called for.

Our Weird Drive to Create Heroes, Even as Christians

One of the most natural things that most of us do with teams and sports figures is to ascribe a greater degree of moral value to them than they actually deserve. For years the Penn State program was upheld (somewhat rightly) as a beacon of everything that was good in the morally compromised, seemingly God-forsaken world of big-time college football. Aside from the occasional bar fight or DUI, the Penn State football program remained mostly scandal-free and boasted above-average graduation rates and almost universally decent kids. And they never messed with their uniforms (bonus).

For the Penn State fan who has papered his basement with team photographs and adorned his body with officially licensed team gear, and who has probably talked for years about how "we do things the right way here," the Sandusky situation really is an occasion for grief. The Penn State posters and officially licensed jerseys are looked at and worn differently in light of what has recently become public.

It should be noted that many fans hang posters and wear licensed apparel of their programs and individual heroes. Northwestern fans say, "At least we have our academic standards." Auburn fans tried to defend Cam Newton's honor (and naiveté) in last year's scandal; and even fans of USC—perhaps the most successful "pro" football team in the history of the Los Angeles media market—defended Reggie Bush's actions (in his own scandal) as the natural reaction of a talented kid and his family being exploited by a cash-cow program.

This deep-seated drive to attach nobility to and defend the programs we love is probably in some weird way proof of our creation in God's image. We want them to be more than football players; we want them to be symbols of something (see: Tebow, Timothy). Tebow's actions have been debated and defended with scary, mouth-frothing intensity by media and fans alike (and the non-Christians are even worse. . . . Okay, not really).

Nothing Good, Apart From Christ

As people ask me about the Penn State situation, two things come to mind, and I'll state them in hopefully the least-pious way possible:

One, I'm sad. Whenever something like this happens, it's an occasion to put aside rooting interests and genuinely feel grieved for all the people involved. But two, I'm reminded of something that we say a lot but I think rarely internalize and actually *live*: the idea that *nothing* good is possible apart from Christ. As proud and hopeful as Penn State football made us feel over the years, this story is an occasion to be reminded that Christ is our *only* comfort and our *only* source of joy. It's a chance to be reminded that God gives football, and sometimes, in His sovereignty, He takes it away.

And I think it's an occasion to question our own tendency toward hero-worship. If we say that we worship the Author and Perfector of our faith, why then do we have an almost insatiable and semi-embarrassing drive to create heroes in other walks of life?

That said, I think we need to keep enjoying our football, but I think we need to enjoy it (like we strive to enjoy all things) with an eye toward the One who makes real joy possible (hint: It's not Tebow).

I'm a sports person—an athlete and a fan. I always have been. As sports people, we're always being disappointed by our heroes, our teammates, and our coaches. Being let down is a part of life. Just this morning I logged on to my computer to find that a guy my age—former Washington State and San Diego Chargers quarterback Ryan Leaf—has been arrested again on drug charges. And then I watched an HBO documentary on legendary boxing trainer Freddie Roach (whom I greatly admire) that basically painted Roach as lonely and miserable in spite of his success. I wasn't surprised, but I was still sad.

These are just small examples of having our faith in something (in this case men, and an institution) shaken. These things (Roach, Sandusky) are hard to see, but they still feel detached and somewhat impersonal because they're not happening to us. The point of those examples is that there is no hope for men, institutions, and enterprises that operate without Christ. Even the most seemingly shining examples of what man can do (like Penn State football pre-scandal) are subject to the fall. It's sad and disappointing for us as observers. It is, of course, worse and harder when we feel that God has abandoned us or, maybe even worse, hates us.

I have felt both of these things at times, and definitely felt it when the trifecta of life (job, fertility, finances) came crashing down on me. I used to have a bad habit of describing things as "God-forsaken" (examples: the Lansing, Michigan, area in the winter, or certain parts of certain cities, among others). I remember feeling that way in Ukraine when we were cold (snowing for what seemed like the fifty-fifth day in a row), alone, and broke. But it couldn't have been further from the truth. God had not only not forsaken us, He was still sovereign, still good, and still working.

God Is Sovereign: Jesus Battles Despondency in the Garden

"If we know that Jesus has already won the battle and defeated sin at the cross," my wife asked recently, "why does Satan keep fighting? Why does he attack us?" It was a good question. I initially responded like I often respond, which is to say, "I don't know." But upon further reflection, it makes sense. I told my wife later that when I was a football player, I was a part of a lot of losing teams. But even in the midst of being on the wrong end of a blowout loss, I still wanted to take a piece out of the opponent. I still wanted the guy across from me to go home feeling beat up and terrible about himself. I wanted to do some damage even though I couldn't change the outcome. The very nature of evil is to want to ruin and destroy good. Satan may or may not know that he's ultimately been defeated at the cross, but either way, he is still prowling about, looking for ways to destroy.

Scripture tells us that Jesus was fully man, but also a man who was in every way without sin. It would follow that if Jesus was fully man, He wasn't some feelingless automaton who didn't experience anything. We know that He felt pain, fear, abandonment, and even the early pangs of despondency in the garden of Gethsemane. Matthew 26:36–38 paints the picture:

> Then Jesus went with them to a place called Gethsemane, and he said to his disciples, "Sit here, while I go over there and pray." And taking with him Peter and the two sons of

Zebedee, he began to be sorrowful and troubled. Then he said to them, "My soul is very sorrowful, even to death; remain here, and watch with me."

Jesus was in the midst of perhaps the most intense spiritual battle ever waged. He was, literally, sweating blood. Satan was trying to produce a spirit of doubt in Jesus—doubt that He was the Savior of mankind, and the feeling that what was about to take place on Calvary would be futile. He was trying to get Jesus to fail in carrying out His task.

But rather than yielding to dark, bitter confusion and despondency, Jesus fights back in a few specific ways. Ways that are extremely helpful and practical for us.

1. Bring your friends. Jesus took Peter and the two sons of Zebedee. Often, for men especially, it's tough to involve our friends in these dark moments. It's hard to rip down the façade and let people in—especially for someone like me, who was raised in the breadbasket of self-sufficiency and quiet, blue-collar determination (the Midwest), and a culture (athletics) where it was looked upon as "soft" to ask for help. Notice that Jesus isn't celebrated here for powering through on His own. The first thing He does is reach out to His friends.

   In the midst of my own "dark night of the soul," I spent a week at a friend's house, allowing him to minister to me just by giving me a quiet place to read and reflect. In the evenings we would sit in his garage, fire up a cigar, and either talk or not talk. I thank God for these times.

2. Be honest. Jesus says that His "soul is very sorrowful, even to death." He leaves nothing to chance and conjecture about how He's feeling and where He's at.

His friends aren't left wondering, "What's wrong with Jesus?" They know because He tells them.

3. Ask for help. Again, Jesus couldn't have been more explicit about this. He said, "Remain here and keep watch with me." Basically He said, "Sit with me so I'm not alone right now." He wanted His friends around, and praying with Him.

   When things were hitting the fan in Ukraine, and when I was losing book deals left and right, I was bitter and I wanted to be alone. I pushed people away. I didn't want people to see me failing and doubting. But when the Holy Spirit pursued me and I began to confess sin, I wanted my close friends and confidants near. There were people in my life, at that time, whom I called daily. I thank God for their help.

4. Go to the Father. Jesus poured out His heart to His Father in prayer. He asked for the cup to be removed in verse 39. Jesus wasn't above asking for a change in circumstances. In this we have a friend and an ally—Jesus felt what we're feeling. It's important to note here that Jesus doesn't just gather His friends around so that He can talk the issue into the ground and obsess about all the details. I've been guilty of this in a HUGE way. I've spent many a night—and many a week—beating conversational dead-horses all over the place. But Jesus immediately goes to His Father in prayer.

5. Rest in sovereignty. Jesus says, "Not as I will, but as you will," in verse 39. He's reaffirming His trust in God's essential *goodness* and in the rightness of God's sovereign plan. Lots of people in my camp (young Reformeddom) are, I think, too quick to skip step 4 and go right to this one, such that if their spouse is dying of cancer they feel somehow sheepish about or afraid of praying for

healing or a drastic change of circumstance. Even Jesus prayed for the removal of the cup in the garden; why shouldn't we? However, He immediately follows that prayer with a reaffirmation of God's sovereignty. So our question is this: Rather than relying on sovereignty as the answer to every difficult question or situation in life, how is our core *belief* in sovereignty driving our reactions to the circumstances in our lives? How is it enabling us to live joyfully and peacefully? How is it enabling us to give and receive grace?

John Piper sums up the battle against despondency in *Future Grace*: "When something drops into your life that seems to threaten your future, remember this: The first shockwaves of the bomb are not sin. The real danger is yielding to them. Giving in. Putting up no spiritual fight. And the root of that surrender is unbelief."[1]

Jesus, of course, does anything but surrender. He trusts in God's sovereignty, but He does it in extremely tangible, practical ways—with friends, by opening up His heart honestly, and by running to the Father.

God Is Working: David Prays Through Fear

Psalm 3 is described as a morning psalm. Interesting, then, that it starts with David describing the number of his many foes. That's a rough way to wake up. And in this case it's not some vague "spiritual" foe—there are real foes pursuing the real David, who is taking flight from those foes.

I was never the kind of guy who would have said that he had enemies. After all, I was a people pleaser—getting everyone to like me was what I did best. But I also spent many years

1. John Piper, *Future Grace* (Colorado Springs: Multnomah Press, 2005), 307.

waking up with a real sense of who wanted something from me and who had seriously made me angry (see: gangster ethics). Publishers. Book critics. Family. People who had disappointed me in some way. In a lot of ways—though I wouldn't have said it at the time—they were foes. Enemies.

A psalm of David.
When he fled from his son Absalom.

> LORD, how many are my foes!
> How many rise up against me!
> Many are saying of me,
> "God will not deliver him."
>
> But you, LORD, are a shield around me,
> my glory, the One who lifts my head high.
> I call out to the LORD,
> and he answers me from his holy mountain.
> (vv. 1–4 NIV)

David uses a lot of battle imagery here as he re-expresses his confidence in God and God alone. It's easy to forget that David started, and made his name, as a soldier. His description of the Lord as a shield is appropriate for us when we are under attack. I used to pray through this psalm when we were in the throes of infertility and my wife was despairing. "Lord, be a shield around her, and lift her head high."

> I lie down and sleep;
> I wake again, because the LORD sustains me.
> I will not fear though tens of thousands
> assail me on every side. (vv. 5–6 NIV)

These two verses mean a great deal to me because I've dealt with insomnia on and off for my whole life. I've tried herbal teas, over-the-counter drugs, prescription drugs, NyQuil (college, not proud of that), late-night television, pacing, and everything else except hitting myself over the head with a hammer, which can even start to sound like a good idea at four in the morning. I've had sleepless nights in loud apartments, quiet apartments, bedrooms that were too hot, too cold, too light, too dark. I've had sleepless nights on several continents. I've resented and been jealous of sleeping people all over the world.

David—though he's being pursued to the death—lies down and sleeps soundly at night. I was listening to an old Tim Keller sermon recently that suggests that the quality of our sleep can sometimes be a barometer of how well we're trusting God. Sleep is a gift from God. And David wakes up determined, in the Lord, to not fear the tens of thousands who assail him. We can pray, and sleep, with the same confidence.

We can also remember, in the midst of great anxiety and physical weakness, the words of the first answer in the Heidelberg Catechism, which read, "I am not my own, but belong—body and soul, in life and in death—to my faithful Savior Jesus Christ . . . He also watches over me in such a way that not a hair can fall from my head without the will of my Father in heaven." It is, as the question suggests, my only comfort in life and death.

> Arise, LORD!
> Deliver me, my God!
> Strike all my enemies on the jaw;
> break the teeth of the wicked.
>
> From the LORD comes deliverance.
> May your blessing be on your people. (vv. 7–8 NIV)

Commentator James Montgomery Boice writes, "The last section is a confident cry for God's deliverance—confident because the Psalmist knows that God has heard him and that God will provide the needed deliverance."[2] In short, David has an unshakable belief that God is *working*.

God Is Good: and You're Not Alone

When we doubt, we're left with two options—curse God and die, or continue to pray, hope, and believe through our doubt. Both sons in the Luke 15 parable of the prodigal son want good things but don't necessarily want their father. The younger son just takes his (cash, inheritance) and runs. And he blows it. He rebels. He goes off the deep end in a huge way. The older son, though, wants the stuff too.

Typically when people hear this story they relate to either the little brother (who has screwed up big time—I relate to him) or the older brother who has, by all appearances, done everything right—because he wants the reward and not necessarily because he loves his father.

The Parable of the Lost Son

There was a man who had two sons. The younger one said to his father, "Father, give me my share of the estate." So he divided his property between them.

Not long after that, the younger son got together all he had, set off for a distant country and there squandered his wealth in wild living. After he had spent everything, there was a severe famine in that whole country, and he began to be in need. So he went and hired himself out to a citizen of that country, who sent him to his fields to feed pigs. He longed to fill his stomach with the pods that the pigs were eating, but no one gave him anything.

2. James M. Boice, *Psalms: An Expositional Commentary, Volume 1* (Grand Rapids, MI: Baker Publishing, 2005), 28.

When he came to his senses, he said, "How many of my father's hired servants have food to spare, and here I am starving to death! I will set out and go back to my father and say to him: Father, I have sinned against heaven and against you. I am no longer worthy to be called your son; make me like one of your hired servants." So he got up and went to his father.

But while he was still a long way off, his father saw him and was filled with compassion for him; he ran to his son, threw his arms around him and kissed him.

The son said to him, "Father, I have sinned against heaven and against you. I am no longer worthy to be called your son."

But the father said to his servants, "Quick! Bring the best robe and put it on him. Put a ring on his finger and sandals on his feet. Bring the fattened calf and kill it. Let's have a feast and celebrate. For this son of mine was dead and is alive again; he was lost and is found." So they began to celebrate.

Meanwhile, the older son was in the field. When he came near the house, he heard music and dancing. So he called one of the servants and asked him what was going on. "Your brother has come," he replied, "and your father has killed the fattened calf because he has him back safe and sound."

The older brother became angry and refused to go in. So his father went out and pleaded with him.

"My son," the father said, "you are always with me, and everything I have is yours. But we had to celebrate and be glad, because this brother of yours was dead and is alive again; he was lost and is found."

Luke 15:11–32

We can, like the younger son, come back and receive our Father's boundless grace. The kid had his story all worked out. He was going to go back home and beg just to be one of his father's hired men. But before he could even get it out of his mouth, his father—a landowner, an aristocrat—bounded off the porch, ran to him, and kissed him. For a wealthy landowner, bounding off the porch and running wasn't something you did. Neither was the unconditional reacceptance and celebration of someone who had shamed you. But the father in this parable does both. This is a picture of God's posture toward us. Isn't this the definition of goodness?

For many years I would have said I understood this goodness. I had read, and even written, books about it. It made sense intellectually. But when I experienced it, it became so much more, well, *good*. The younger son is humbled enough to accept a grace that is, by all accounts, extremely counterintuitive. It doesn't make sense to the older brother, who broods outside the feast with a chip on his shoulder. I lived like this for too many years. But when I was finally humbled enough to receive grace, my entire outlook changed. The way I talked. The way I thought through issues. The way I treated my wife and kids. I began to live like someone who had been pardoned rather than someone who was entitled and thought it was God's job to hook him up.

Rather, as Christians, we live lives full of knowledge, conviction, and gratitude, and out of that gratitude flows joy. Answer 21 of the Heidelberg Catechism describes this true faith: "True faith is not only a knowledge and conviction that everything God reveals in his Word is true; it is also a deep-rooted assurance, created in me by the Holy Spirit, through the gospel, that, out of sheer grace earned for us by Christ, not only others, but I too, have had my sins forgiven, have been made forever right with God, and have been granted salvation."

Starting Your Life Again

Jerry Maguire is one of my favorite movies. In fact, I write about it way too much, which is something you might already have noticed and maybe even been annoyed by if you read my work at all. One of my favorite scenes (I have many) takes place at the beginning, when Jerry is in his hotel room in Miami, having the epiphany that he's lived a self-centered, self-serving, small life. He shivers, horrified at his life, in a darkened hotel room. He's sweating. He gets up and sits at his laptop. He's convicted of his guilt, and in the film he writes a memo ("It's a mission statement") outlining the changes he's going to make, and how it will impact his business and ultimately his life. It will, he hopes, make him a new person. "Even the cover looked like *The Catcher in the Rye*," he explains. Then Jerry Cantrell from Soundgarden, playing the guy at the twenty-four-hour Kinko's counter, has a classic line about "how you become great."

I've watched the movie repeatedly at different stages of my life over the past fifteen years. We watched it in the theater on our honeymoon in 1996, shortly after the film's release, and connected with the love story between Jerry and Dorothy Boyd. When I was a professional athlete for one season, I related most to Rod Tidwell. At various times I've related to Jerry's speech in the airport where he implores Rod to take his jacket, because he's "finished . . . cloaked in failure." The film, for us, is cinematic comfort food—good and just relatable enough to hold our attention, but somehow comfortable and familiar at the same time.

When at thirty-five I was confronted with the sinful state of my heart, like Jerry, I spent a few days in a dark room, sweating and lamenting the condition of my soul. I felt helpless, but I felt like I was having a profound experience with the Holy Spirit. The experience was physical as well as mental and emotional. I couldn't eat. I slept less and less each night. I shivered as though I had a fever, but every time I took my temperature it registered 98.6 degrees.

The release came with confession of sin and a repentant heart. I had spent my entire life in church, and yet I'd spent my entire life feeling sorry for and even guilty for things. I was aware, in a broad sense, that I was a sinner. But I had never before done the hard work of true repentance, and I had never had the experience of trusting God, moment to moment, for my hope and peace. Repentance is the only way to true joy because it's such a fundamental part of the Gospel. "Repentance," wrote Puritan Thomas Brooks, "is the vomit of the soul." John Piper writes in *Future Grace*, "But if you would turn from self as the source of satisfaction (= repentance), and come to Jesus for enjoyment of all that God is for us in him (= faith), then the itch (for human glory) would be replaced by a well of water springing up to eternal life."[3] So it's only natural that a book on doubt/ struggle would end here. At repentance. At joy.

In a sense, I had finally started my life.

My new favorite scene in *Jerry Maguire* is the immediate aftermath of the furious night of writing in the hotel room, after he produces his magnum opus, called "The Things We Think But Do Not Say: The Future of Our Business." Maguire says, "I was thirty-five, and I had just started my life. I was my father's son again."

I remember what it felt like to be my father's son, sitting with him in that darkened den, watching a football game together—feeling a mix of elation (to be with him), complete safety and security, total honesty, and an unbridled hope for the future. It was what innocence and childlikeness *felt* like. As an adult, I grieved the fact that I would probably never feel that again—that life had become a series of grievances, sins, and disappointments that I just had to weather quietly, because that was the "manly" thing to do.

3. John Piper, *Future Grace* (Colorado Springs: Multnomah Press, 2005), 94.

Repentance, and receiving grace, has allowed me to *give* grace in abundance. We give grace out of gratitude, and we live our lives in a passionate pursuit of Christ because of what He *did* for us, the worst of sinners. Like Jerry Maguire, at thirty-five I have started my life again.

And I am my Father's son.

8

The God Who Finds Us

RONNIE MARTIN

There are few stories in the Bible more heartbreaking than the story of Adam and Eve. There's a poetic, otherworldly, and almost mystical quality about it that not only stimulates our imaginations but also tugs at the longing of our heart. From the initial impression one gets from the text, Adam and Eve's idyllic time in the garden of Eden feels incredibly brief. God created Adam, laid out his job description, and then put him to work as the world's first zoology and horticulture expert. Since being productive in the workplace wasn't enough to satisfy Adam's needs, God created an equal yet better-looking version of him to help complete the picture. So let's get this straight:

They lived in a garden paradise.
Their bodies were in a state of perfect health.
They were naked together, all day.

They lived with lions, tigers, and bears without getting mauled to death and eaten.

They took walks with God in the garden.

Okay, you'd have to be the most hardened, bitter, un-fun person in the world to not want the life they had. It sadly ended up not being enough, however.

> Now the serpent was more crafty than any other beast of the field that the LORD God had made. He said to the woman, "Did God actually say, 'You shall not eat of any tree in the garden'?" And the woman said to the serpent, "We may eat of the fruit of the trees in the garden, but God said, 'You shall not eat of the fruit of the tree that is in the midst of the garden, neither shall you touch it, lest you die.'" But the serpent said to the woman, "You will not surely die. For God knows that when you eat of it your eyes will be opened, and you will be like God, knowing good and evil." So when the woman saw that the tree was good for food, and that it was a delight to the eyes, and that the tree was to be desired to make one wise, she took of its fruit and ate, and she also gave some to her husband who was with her, and he ate. Then the eyes of both were opened, and they knew that they were naked. And they sewed fig leaves together and made themselves loincloths.
>
> Genesis 3:1–7

There comes a moment in all of our lives when our eyes are opened to the reality of who we are, what we've done, and what we've gained or lost in the process. For Adam and Eve, it came as the result of direct disobedience to God, in which their minds and hearts were plunged into a state of darkness that altered the existence of mankind for all eternity.

Their initial reactions are peculiar, to say the least. The first was one of self-awareness: They realized that, lo and behold, they had been *naked* all this time. The second went from reaction to action: They made clothes to cover themselves.

We're not given any insight into the kind of heart wrenching anguish they might have been experiencing following their act of disobedience. We don't know what kind of behavior they displayed in their attempts to frantically sew together something to wear. Up to this point, there'd been no need to break out the old sewing machine and stitch together some new threads. There's no record of the conversation they may have had after eating the fruit. Was Eve upset? Crying? Or was she angry with herself for being so easily deceived by the serpent? Was Adam angry? Was he humiliated for giving in to his wife? Was he plotting revenge? Did he feel disgusted at how easily he was seduced by a piece of fruit? One thing we do know is that all those sinful thoughts and emotions were now possible because sin had entered their hearts.

And they heard the sound of the LORD God walking in the garden in the cool of the day, and the man and his wife hid themselves from the presence of the LORD God among the trees of the garden. But the LORD God called to the man and said to him, "Where are you?" And he said, "I heard the sound of you in the garden, and I was afraid, because I was naked, and I hid myself." He said, "Who told you that you were naked? Have you eaten of the tree of which I commanded you not to eat?" The man said, "The woman whom you gave to be with me, she gave me fruit of the tree, and I ate." Then the LORD God said to the woman, "What is this that you have done?" The woman said, "The serpent deceived me, and I ate."

Genesis 3:8–13

A couple of things unfolded for Adam and Eve as new sinners in desperate need of a Savior.

1. They Heard God and Hid

We always have two choices when our sin has been exposed: retreat to God or run from Him. Here's the thing: Running runs us into the ground. Running caused Adam and Eve to invent ways to cover their own sin, which for them was breaking out the thread and needle and getting dressed as soon as possible. Our sin always causes us to have to DO something when we move in any direction other than God, which by the way, is exhausting and fruitless. Retreating to God is just that. It's seeing God as a place of refuge. It's not manic, frantic movement. It's stopping! It's confessing that we have chosen darkness over light and that we want God to illuminate our hearts once again with the revealing light of His forgiveness. It's a plea for rest. Adam and Eve experienced no rest as they started multitasking their way toward covering their indiscretion.

2. They Saw God and Were Ashamed

It's interesting that when God asked Adam where he was, he said he was hiding because he was naked. Doesn't it say that before God visited them they had sewn leaves together to clothe themselves? Why was Adam afraid of his nakedness when he had gone to all that trouble to put some clothes on and he wasn't naked anymore? The answer is that he *was* naked. Although he put clothes on his body, his heart was still naked and exposed. There was nothing Adam could do in his own power to cover the shame and nakedness that he was experiencing before an all-holy, all-perfect God. Worse yet, in his sinful, spineless passivity, he ratted out his own wife. Instead of protecting and shielding her from the deceit of the serpent, he now blamed her for his own fall from grace.

As a new but accomplished sinner, Adam tried to conceal his sin, but his sin was faithful to reveal his faithlessness and disloyalty to his wife.

In spite of all of this, God did the most remarkable thing. He found them. God sought Adam and Eve out. He called for them while they were cowering in their ridiculous, not-so-secret hiding place. He cared about them, confronted them, and gave them the opportunity to confess to Him. And even when they didn't, He promised He would help them anyway. Even before God created Adam and Eve and the world they lived in, He had a plan already on file to save them. It's just like the Lord to do this. Our struggles come from our fallenness. We enter into doubt and despair because at some point we believed a lie instead of the truth. At some point we believed that God's goodness wasn't so good and that His greatness wasn't so grand. Somehow, in the shallowness of our minds, we believed that we're the ones who should have control over the destiny of our lives, only to realize that when we arrive at our destination, when we eat of the forbidden fruit, the result is disappointment, fear, and shame. What we need to understand is that when we do arrive at that place of self-imposed destiny, God is already there. There's never a moment so dark that God can lose sight of where we are. The brightness of His glory cuts through the density of our darkness every time.

> I will put enmity between you and the woman, and between your offspring and her offspring; he shall bruise your head, and you shall bruise his heel.
>
> Genesis 3:15

God promised and provided. He didn't let Adam and Eve wander around the garden for the next day, week, month, or year sinking deeper and deeper into their darkness, despair, and sin. Even as they made no attempt to confront and confess to God everything they had done, God willingly came to them with a plan that would restore everything they had lost just moments before. This is the God who finds us. This is the character and heart of the One who will never fail in His endeavors to bring whom He chooses back to himself. He will seek us out, search our hearts, and see us through the high waters of hell to reveal the greatness of His glory. How does this look for those of us who didn't commit a sin that changed the face of the world? The same, because the sins we commit now are equal to the ones that changed the face of the world. And God's response? That never changes either.

> The steadfast love of the LORD never ceases;
>   his mercies never come to an end;
> they are new every morning;
>   great is your faithfulness.
> "The LORD is my portion," says my soul,
>   "therefore I will hope in him."
>   Lamentations 3:22–24

Elijah: The Defeat of Victory

Much is made of the prophet Elijah's descent into despondency following his gig on Mount Carmel against the false priests of Israel. Elijah's victory is the stuff of legends. After calling out the opposing team to a challenge of faith and fire in which they spectacularly failed, Elijah brings the show home with a display of pyrotechnics courtesy of the hand of God. Not only did Elijah win against a team that outnumbered him 450 to 1, but he also got to slaughter every last one of them as the prize for his victory. But wait, there's more. First it started to rain again after a three-year drought that Elijah had prophesied would happen. Secondly, God turned him into The Flash by blessing him with superhuman speed to beat King Ahab home in his chariot. Call me crazy, but that sounds like a pretty good day for our boy Elijah. In fact, most prophets I know would be chest-bumping everyone from here to Louisiana after a day like that. So what happened to Elijah?

After he gets back to the palace of Jezreel where wicked Queen Jezebel was staying, she sends him a quick note saying that he would be dead by the next day if she had anything to say about it, and she kind of did.

Granted, not a fun piece of news to get after such a thrilling day, but it sounds familiar, doesn't it? I remember how often in life I've had wonderful days followed by what feels like the worst ones ever. Or words of discouragement that come immediately after an encouraging or hopeful word. Sometimes it seems like the second we achieve even a moment's victory, there's a crushing blow of defeat around the corner waiting to swallow it up. A glass-half-empty view? Maybe. Or maybe God is so concerned about the devastating effects of pride swelling in our hearts that He allows crushing defeats and blows to our egos to serve as acts of mercy and grace. Never-ending victories would create disastrous results in the hearts and minds of God's people, which is why you'll never meet a Christian who has never suffered loss, however great or small.

After Elijah received that wonderful piece of news from Jezebel, it tells us that he was afraid and ran for his life to the wilderness. He sat down under a tree and asked the Lord if he could die. The discouragement that Elijah felt at that moment was overwhelming. It didn't matter that he was coming off a day that would go down in history as one of God's most dazzling displays of victory over false religions and idol worship. What ultimately didn't happen was changed hearts, which was the one thing that Elijah desired above all else. The fact is that sometimes we don't see circumstances change. Sometimes we don't get the joy and privilege of seeing people's hearts turned to Christ from the work that God does through our efforts. But the circumstance of our heart can change. In fact, we can see God mold and shape our hearts in more profound ways when they're hurting than when they're not.

But God doesn't leave Elijah to sink into further self-consumption. He doesn't grant Elijah's request to die. What He does do is graciously meet him in the depths of his despair, and asks him this question: "What are you doing here, Elijah?" Here's what he replies:

> I have been very jealous for the LORD, the God of hosts. For the people of Israel have forsaken your covenant, thrown down your altars, and killed your prophets with the sword, and I, even I only, am left, and they seek my life, to take it away.
>
> 1 Kings 19:10

It was true. Elijah had spent his life jealously seeking the true God of Israel above all others and calling the people to turn their hearts back to Him. He had tried and he had failed, but God still came to him in both his faithfulness and failure. When God calls us to do a faithful work for Him, He also provides the results. We act, but only the Holy Spirit can activate. It's when we think that we're responsible for the activation of people's hearts that we start to despair and ask what good it did to even act at all. The Lord's response is telling. He didn't tell Elijah what a fantastic job he had done and that there was no reason for him to have such low self-esteem issues. He doesn't give him a ten-step list on finding true self-worth. No, that would've kept Elijah's focus on Elijah. Instead, He reveals himself to Elijah in a low whisper, illustrating that although He acts in overwhelming and spectacular ways like He did on Mount Carmel, He also reveals himself in stillness and solitude, while through it all, His sovereign plan continues to unfold. For Elijah's future, God's sovereign plan was threefold.

1. He got to hand off his ministry to his successor, Elisha, knowing that the work God started in him would continue.
2. Instead of God granting his request to die on Mount Horeb, he sends a chariot of fire to pick him up and bring him home. Nice trade-off, I'm thinking.
3. Years later, on the Mount of Transfiguration, God shows Elijah His plan to redeem His people through the work of Jesus Christ.

What an amazingly intricate, gracious and caring plan that God unfolded for Elijah! He didn't just find the guy during a low moment, hit him upside the head, tell him everything was going to be okay, and to just buck up already. No, He met him where he was at, reminded him of who he was, and then had him carry on with the plan that He had already established. Here's the thing: We don't know if Elijah ended well. We don't get much insight into whether there was any sort of shift or lift in his heart after the incident on Mount Horeb. What we do see is a God who didn't leave him alone, ministered to his physical needs, and put him back on the mission He called him to. What we do see is a man who obeyed when God told him to act, in spite of how downcast he felt. The result? Elijah saw God. He saw God work in spite of his disappointment and struggle. Was God working in the way that Elijah would've preferred? Doesn't look like it, but we remember from Isaiah 55:8 that "my thoughts are not your thoughts, neither are your ways my ways, declares the LORD." That's good news for us when we consider where our choices and preferences in the midst of dark times might take us.

Where our vision is clouded, unclear, and easily bended by the erratic nature of our emotions, God's is not. His vision is always clear, always accurate, and never swayed by human emotions. His immutability (that He does not change) is one of our great hopes and promises.

> For I the LORD do not change. . . .
> Malachi 3:6

There was a reason why God chose to use Elijah the way He did, and that Elijah wouldn't get to see the fruition of his labor until after his death. Is that supposed to encourage us? Actually . . . yes. It means that we act, but He handles the activation. It means that we can take that rather large anvil off our shoulders knowing that every move we make, every emotion we feel, every defeat we experience, every doubt we harbor, and every disappointment we carry is *all* under the sovereign control of God. *All* of it.

Partially Sovereign

If we're honest—and most of us aren't—the majority of us actually believe in the partial sovereignty of God. Sure, we say we trust in His goodness, believe He has a plan for us, and probably pray for greater faith in Him, but our lives tell a different story. If people could read our thoughts, feel our emotions, and know our motivations, they'd probably question if we believe in any of this at all. We throw around the phrase "God is in control" like peanut shells at a baseball game, but as soon as something feels out of our control, we panic like cats at a dog show. Here's a stark yet beautifully liberating reality: We don't control anything. We never have, we never will. Because God is sovereign, it means He has perfect control over all things. No boundaries, no limitations. All-knowing, all-loving. There is no place in this universe where His presence does not exist. There is nothing that can happen in this entire universe without His knowledge and consent.

So breathe a sigh of relief. He has this thing. He's our only hope from losing hope.

One of the great, modern hymns of our time, "How Deep the Father's Love for Us," reminds us of Christ's love, His sovereignty, and what He came to accomplish for us. Our lack of faith, disappointments, and struggles to believe in God's plans for us? They were all accounted for on the cross by a God who was and is in control of all things.

To Lighten Our Darkness

What shade of darkness is surrounding your life today? Maybe there are some severe realities from your past that have caused you to struggle to believe in God's goodness for the future. Maybe you don't carry around any dark secrets or weighty tragedies from the past but still feel like you are walking under a black cloud of mild despair and nagging doubt.

What's interesting about doubt and despair is that they cause our focus to center on the very thing that God wants us to stop focusing on: ourselves. He knows that ever since Adam and Eve shifted the desire they originally had for God over to themselves, we inherited something we would struggle with our entire lives. Us. It's this self-consuming focus on *us* that ultimately casts a dark shadow of doubt over our hearts and minds. And the world tells us this is a good thing. How many times a day do we hear these lines?

I need to do what's right for *me*.

I deserve some *me* time.

I need to focus on *myself.*
I need to learn to love *myself.*

When we as believers struggle to believe, it's not that we've misplaced hope, it's that we've misplaced God, who is our hope. We've traded the desire and affection we're supposed to have for God with a desire and affection for self. It's a repeat episode of Adam and Eve. We find ourselves unclothed, afraid, and ashamed, living in doubt of God's promises and in denial of His goodness. But God finds us and restores our hope in only Him. When we find ourselves under a cover of darkness, God doesn't just hand us flashlights so we can see our way around without tripping over everything. No, He consumes the darkness with His light! He illuminates those areas in our lives so that we are not hidden under darkness any longer but "hidden with Christ in God" (Colossians 3:3).

He wouldn't be God if He did anything less.

> For you are my lamp, O LORD, and my God lightens my darkness.
>
> 2 Samuel 22:29

Look around and see what lamps are lighting your life. We constantly have the dim lights of careers, relationships, hobbies, kids, and homes threatening to replace the all-consuming and all-illuminating light of Christ in our lives. These dim lights ultimately burn out because they were never meant to be the ultimate source of light in our lives.

In these times, our prayer needs to be like David's in the Psalms, when he was hiding for his life in a cave from King Saul:

> Be merciful to me, O God, be merciful to me,
>   for in you my soul takes refuge;

in the shadow of your wings I will take refuge,
  till the storms of destruction pass by.
I cry out to God Most High,
  to God who fulfills his purpose for me.
He will send from heaven and save me;
  he will put to shame him who tramples on me.
    Selah
God will send out his steadfast love and his
  faithfulness!

Psalm 57:1–3

Like He did for David, God will fulfill His own purpose in us. He will transfer our selfish gaze back to His selfless ways. He will provide us with joyful reassurance in our darkest times of doubt and wondering. He will show us mercy in the dark solitude of our storms and become the great refuge for our sorrowful souls when we repent of our self-sufficiency and return to the shadow of His wings. We will once again feel the strength and security of His steadfast love and be reminded of His never-ending faithfulness. He will lighten the depths of our darkness with the lamp of His transcendent love, and we will see ever more clearly the goodness of His grace and the greatness of His glory.

We will once again have hope in Christ, our only hope.

Ronnie Martin is on staff at Ashland Grace Church and enjoys writing, preaching, teaching, and speaking. He is married to wife Melissa, and they have one daughter. Follow Ronnie on Twitter @ronniejmartin.

Ted Kluck is a freelance writer. He has written several books, and his work has appeared in such places as *ESPN the Magazine* and *Christianity Today*. Ted mentored a young man with a prison record and wrote about it in his book *Dallas and the Spitfire*. Ted lives in Grand Ledge, Michigan, with his wife and two sons.

Discipleship Isn't a Program, It's a Relationship

Ted is a thirty-four-year-old father of two who's been going to church his whole life. Dallas is a twenty-one-year-old with a troubled past and a prison record. When they agree to meet regularly for "discipleship," they know that chatting once a week in a coffee shop just won't cut it. Restoring an old Triumph Spitfire is more their style.

This is not "12 Steps to Mentoring a Man for Christ" or "The Blockhead's Guide to Discipleship." This is real life. It's the true story of a guy a lot like you and another guy nothing at all like you. It shows how real men can be friends with one another and get closer to Jesus. It isn't easy. It isn't a checklist. If you have a rigid system in place, you're doing it wrong. It's all about living life for others.

Dallas and the Spitfire by Ted Kluck and Dallas Jahncke

BETHANYHOUSE

Stay up-to-date on your favorite books and authors with our *free* e-newsletters. Sign up today at bethanyhouse.com.

Find us on Facebook.